Attachment Parenting

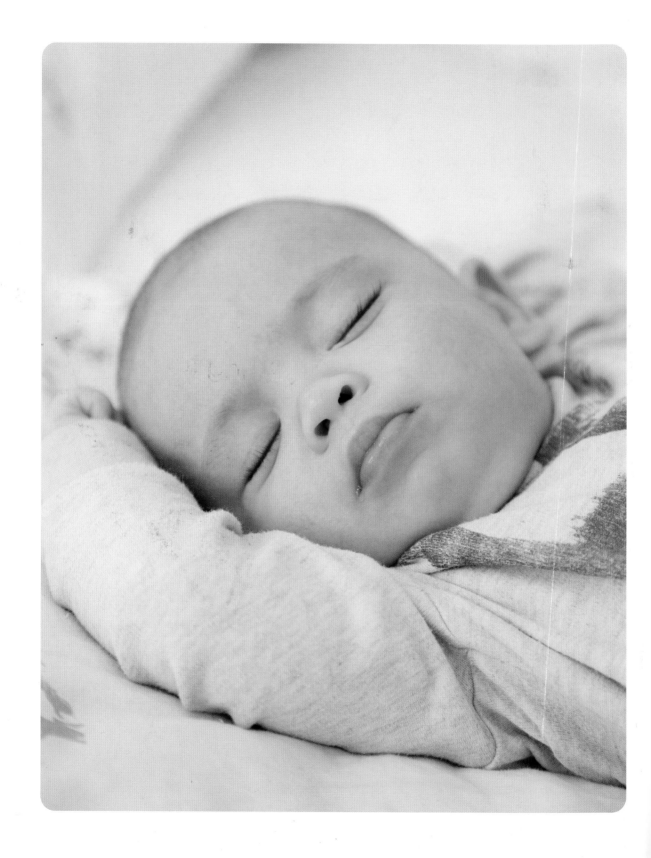

Attachment Parenting

Advice, Tips, and Solutions for Caring for Your Baby

LACIE RADER

CICO BOOKS

LONDON NEW YORK

Published in 2014 by CICO Books

An imprint of Ryland Peters & Small Ltd

20–21 Jockey's Fields,   519 Broadway, 5th Floor

London WC1R 4BW   New York, NY 10012

www.rylandpeters.com

10 9 8 7 6 5 4 3 2 1

Please note that the advice in this book is not intended to be considered
as a substitute for medical advice from your family doctor or any other
qualified medical practitioner. Neither the author nor the publisher can
be held responsible for any claim arising out of the use or misuse of
suggestions made in this book.

A CIP catalog record for this book is available from the Library of
Congress and the British Library.

ISBN: 978-1-78249-109-5

Printed in China

Editor: Nicky Gyopari
Designer: Emily Breen
Photographers: Emma Mitchell, Penny Wincer
Illustrator: Hannah George

For digital editions, visit www.cicobooks.com/apps.php

Contents

Introduction

Attachment Parenting: How this Book Approaches It

Attachment Parenting is for individuals who are sensitive to gentle, natural, and simple parenting methods. The book is based on Attachment Parenting (AP,) a style of caring for your infant created by Dr. William Sears. He believes that when children's needs for touch and emotional bonding are fully met, no matter how intense that need is, they develop into secure and happy adults.

Dr. Sears defines this parenting style using seven principles, sometimes also known as the seven "Bs" of Attachment Parenting: birth bonding, breast-feeding, bedding close to baby, babywearing, belief in the value of your baby's cries, balance, and being wary

of baby training that suggests you encourage your child's independence with rigid or extreme parenting styles such as crying-it-out.

This book provides solutions to the challenges that all parents face, but it differs from other parenting guides in that the tips here adhere to the seven principles above. It is written in the belief that readers are confident in their decision to Attachment Parent. You will find very little in the way of the benefits of Attachment Parenting or the debate between conventional and AP parents. I believe that once a parent decides to practice Attachment Parenting, it's important to be beyond the debate.

However, it is sometimes difficult for AP parents to move beyond the debate, and I believe there are several reasons for this:

※ Parenting theories are strict—resulting in heated debates, tears, and broken friendships, all resulting in defensive feelings.

※ Feelings of doubt—AP parents honestly begin to doubt their methods because the challenges are so difficult, especially if other AP parents are not supportive and open about their experiences. New AP parents wonder if they are doing something wrong or whether this parenting style actually works.

※ Criticism from other, non-AP parents—this naturally breeds self-doubt. While it is commendable to be open-minded, it's important to notice the difference between being flexible and being controlled by anxiety. Being open-minded should contribute to positive parenting experiences.

I'm assuming that you don't want another pat on the back or rant about why this parenting method is superior. I'm guessing you'd rather bypass statistics and an index of AP terms and get straight to business. You have conviction. You know that it's hard work and you've signed up for it. Maybe you want to be more prepared than others before you; maybe you are in the thick of it now. Wherever you are at, Attachment Parenting is intended for you.

Challenges and solutions

Having conviction doesn't make everything easier. In some ways, it makes parenting more difficult. You have an idea of how you want to do everything but as you're doing it, you begin to realize it's harder than you imagined it would be, and sometimes your conviction will be tested. You need answers about why it's harder than you expected and you need tips to help make things easier. You need someone to confide in, because everyone else you have spoken to is either against your parenting methods

or so in favor of them that they refuse to expose the difficult aspects of it to you.

When I address certain parenting challenges, it may seem as though I'm blaming Attachment Parenting for the challenge or for making the solution to the problem more difficult. One may even conclude that I am against some aspects of Attachment Parenting. I want to be very clear from the beginning that I am not against any aspect of Attachment Parenting. Please do not mistake my openness about how difficult it has been for me for regret or disappointment; I would do it all over again in a second.

You also need someone to share the joys of AP with. You need examples of challenging times that resulted in moments of triumph and other parenting successes. You need to hear about the endless opportunities for bonding and emotional growth that you and your child will share because of your parenting style. You need to be reminded that all of this work is a manifestation of your ability to experience love, compassion, and empathy, and you will get all of that and more in the following pages.

Attachment Parenting is honest and straightforward but also optimistic and solution focused. I have given my whole heart to keeping my child happy and healthy. In writing this book, I want to help you in your endeavor. This book contains hundreds of Attachment Parenting friendly tips with the hope that you will find something that works for your family's unique needs. The solutions here are everything an Attachment Parent needs: gentle, creative, practical, detailed, honest, reflective, sympathetic, inexpensive—and humorous.

Attachment Parenting:
The Good, The Bad, and The Ugly

Attachment Parents are often on the receiving end of statements such as, "He'll never sleep alone," "That's why she's so needy," "Neither of you are getting enough sleep," and "You won't be a good mother if you're too tired or selfless to be happy." This section is for all those who are on the receiving end of these statements and are being put in a position where they have to defend their practices.

When speaking with parents who feel compelled to remind you that you're making a rod for your own back, I recommend explaining that you agree. You're not just making a rod; you're carving it, polishing it, and making it perfect. If we, as Attachment Parents, confessed to the feeling that yes, there is a bit of a rod in our backs, then we might hear about it less often. After all, it's called Attachment Parenting because the end result is that your child is "attached." And along with the many wonderful aspects of your child's attachment comes the inevitable hard work.

Other parents probably have good intentions. They hate seeing us suffer so much, but we already know that we'd be happier if we hired a babysitter, went out more often, and slept with our monitors turned off. We know that our methods get in the way of restful sleep and we know that our methods may cause clinginess in the early years of our child's life. We've considered it all; we simply believe that this is what's best for our children.

To those of you who are about to embark upon Attachment Parenting, while you shouldn't be scared off by the remarks of other parents, you also shouldn't dismiss them. No parenting style is free from its unique challenges. Attachment Parenting is not always enjoyable and it's certainly not easy. Some of the practices can result in habits that are difficult to break, and should you experience this, please be assured that you're not doing something wrong.

My advice is always to take solace in knowing that you're not alone and being able to say, "It very well may be my parenting style but it's worth it to me." We have to have this sort of conviction because the good (your child's emotional well-being) will far outweigh the bad.

The Good

Please note, I am not suggesting that any of the following is untrue about other parenting methods. It is important to recognize that all parenting methods share some positive results and that none are flawless.

* Your child knows that you are always there for him.
* You don't have to worry about correlations between neural development delays and crying it out.
* You feel at peace by following your parenting instincts.
* Your child is happy.
* Your child does not cry often or for long periods of time.
* Your child will be able to ask for whatever he needs.
* Your child will feel free to express any emotion that he is experiencing.
* Your child learns right from wrong without being afraid to do what is wrong.
* Earlier cognitive development is revealed in children who have the sort of intensive engagement that AP provides.
* Your methods will build security, self-esteem, and independence in your child.
* Your child will not hear "no" as much and will learn that he is respected (and in turn will be cooperative.)

The Bad and The Ugly

These are my experiences, friends' experiences, and the experiences of mothers I've gotten to know on parenting forums. This is not science but real life. If you relate to the points below, you may find relief in knowing that there are others like you. If none of it relates to you, you can feel very fortunate.

* Attachment Parenting is hard work and can be draining.
* Your child may not sleep without you for many years, thus affecting your sleep.
* Your child may not get used to being with other people; you might not get breaks.
* Your child is used to having his needs met and may be emotionally expressive or demanding.
* Your child will get used to you being there for any and all upsets (this is exhausting.)
* Your child may want to nurse on demand for years. At some point, this gets frustrating and is exhausting.
* Your child may be clingy and not want to leave your arms during outings.
* Your child may be impatient.

My Story

In February of 2010, my husband and I learned that we were going to be parents. Our daughter was due and born on Halloween. Short of a terrible first trimester, we had a wonderful pregnancy and we thought we had it all together. We had purchased all of the baby paraphernalia, the nursery was complete with a folded wardrobe, we had been calling her by her chosen name for months, and we had a plan for work and finances arranged so that I could stay at home. I learned how to labor, breastfeed, babywear, and co-sleep, or rather, I learned as much as I could without actually having any experience. We believed we were prepared but somehow, even though all of our preparations were supposed to qualify us to take care of a newborn, they didn't.

I am now convinced that no amount of baby paraphernalia and study prepares you for becoming a parent for the first time. If you have a child, you already know that part of our story. No one is fully prepared to take care of their first newborn. For one thing, your brain can't conceive of the absurdity that is a newborn's schedule. While it's true

that newborns sometimes sleep up to sixteen hours a day, someone forgot to tell us that it was possible for them both to sleep sixteen hours and wake up sixteen times in the same day. For some parents, this may correspond with sixteen daily scenarios where your baby is crying desperately to be spared from her own exhaustion.

Always on call

A new mother is tired because her baby sleeps more in one day than her mother sleeps in a week. A baby's feeding schedule can be similarly unpredictable. Babies don't nurse at the same three times each day, but, rather, they nurse for two minutes at a time, or an hour at a time. Such challenges are difficult for all parents, but I would argue that they are even more challenging for the Attachment Parent. Attachment Parents are dedicated to soothing their children through sleep issues and clinginess. We answer each of our newborn's cries by responding with food, cuddles, and singing; we do it consistently, promptly, at anytime of the day, regardless of our own current state or needs. Our tend-to-baby button is tireless and limitless.

Then there are the babies with conditions such as colic, high sensitivity, food allergies, clinginess, and high need, which will even further surprise a new parent. Most new parents will have trouble in one or two of these areas to some degree. Some parents will have all of these troubles in varying degrees— that would be us, the Raders. Except that the degree of extremity didn't vary much. Rather, it hovered over each challenge, remaining extreme most of the time. In *Attachment Parenting*, I look in detail at all of these more specialized topics, as well as give in-depth insights into the most commonly shared challenges of taking care of a baby and toddler, all based on my own firsthand experience and solutions.

It is normal to find yourself unprepared and frustrated as you come to terms with the reality that, at least temporarily, the execution of daily activities such as eating, using your hands, showering, and peeing will be impossible. This is a normal phase because all new parents go through it. Then there are other realities that some parents are faced with, far worse than I could ever imagine. My heart goes out to these parents and in light of them my complaints pale in comparison. Nevertheless, our little family's experience with our firstborn was not exactly normal.

Our high-need daughter

Keli is a "high-need" child. I've since come to adopt the term "highly sensitive" as it seems more appropriate when referring to toddlers. She fits all of Dr. Sears' twelve qualities of a high-need baby. Too often, in response to my declarations about how hard things were at home, people would say, "That's normal for babies." If that were true, Sears, a pediatrician and father of eight children, would not have had a reason to develop this term to describe Hayden, one of his children. Most of the people who assumed Keli was a normal baby hadn't spent more than thirty minutes with her. They didn't realize that those thirty minutes were preceded by many hours of preparation so that she would be happy for half an hour when we had company.

It all began with the discovery that Keli would only sleep if she were lying on me. I slept on the couch every night for two months with her on my chest . I learned to contort my body into bizarre positions so that Keli and I could both get some much-needed sleep. She couldn't be put down throughout the day much either. Well-intentioned friends told me it was okay to her let her cry a little, so I tried that, but due to her sensitive nature, a little cry turned into hysteria in just a few minutes. As it turned out, it wasn't okay, not for us at least. Whenever I tried this,

it became evident that I had trapped myself into a long and draining soothe-Keli-fest in order to restore some peace. And it wasn't just around sleep or not wanting to be put down—she cried when being dressed, having diapers changed, having a bath. It was all equally stressful.

Turning detective

Then came the endless speculation as to why our child was so difficult. We speculated that perhaps she was high need because of a difficult, long labor that caused her stress and was followed by some time in the hospital. Then, around twelve weeks after she was born, poor health symptoms surfaced. We began to wonder if she wasn't "just clingy." As you know, if you have read a baby book or asked a doctor what a breast-fed baby stool should look like, there's no clear-cut answer. Whatever you tell them, they will tell you it's normal. Our doctors said that her six to seven liquid stools a day were normal. Turns out they were not. We also assumed spitting up was normal for newborns, no matter how excessive. Turns out it's not.

After many long nights of Keli's intense screaming and carrying her around the house, I became

certain our daughter was in pain. I didn't care that babies before her had gone through this; that didn't make it normal. Most people would have described what we were going through as colic and, yes, that would be true. She did have colic. But what is colic? It's only a list of symptoms, and I already had that list of symptoms before I had the term colic. I wanted to know why she had colic; in other words, why was my daughter in pain? I needed to know so that I could help her. It took a lot of research but eventually I came to realize that reflux was causing her pain and that food allergies were causing her reflux. We initiated an elimination diet (the one recommended by Sears) and the colic subsided in just three weeks.

Life with Keli soon became easier. People used to compliment us all the time on how happy she was because she was a smiley, cheerful, engaging delight. I would explain to them that we worked extraordinarily hard for this. Keli was either ecstatic or distraught. She was rarely easygoing or neutral. To keep her from being distraught meant sleeping beside her, nursing her constantly, holding her most of the day, not leaving her with anyone else, teaching her new things, keeping her away from situations and people that were too stimulating, to name but a few. If we ever failed to do this, we were met with a meltdown. Sometimes it would go into the next day.

Meltdowns

Most people can't imagine what a meltdown looks like. The same people that would push us into trying new ways with her regarding handling clingy situations would sit back humbled and concerned for her when they realized the intense emotional effect following their advice had on our child. I made a point of making sure that certain people saw this, because they were close to her and I needed them to be fully aware that Keli's needs were not the same as that of other babies. I now have a small group of loving friends and family that I trust understand Keli and our chosen methods for taking care of her. I am thankful for those who gave us understanding, support, and sympathy during that first year.

Learning how to cope

We had to find new ways to deal with Keli's meltdowns that went even beyond our AP strategies of co-sleeping, holding, and nursing. We were met, as I mentioned earlier, with true emotional meltdowns for things such as baths, diaper changes, hair brushing, getting dressed, and just being in the car—and had to find ways to deal with this. This wasn't a behavioral response, but a truly intense emotional reaction to her surroundings. If you have a sensitive child, you will understand this. Dr. Elizabeth Pantley, who wrote *The No-Cry Sleep Solution,* acknowledges that what crying is for one child may be something completely different for the more sensitive child. A parent needs to be tuned into different types of crying.

During all of this, I was frantic to learn how to make our lives easier. I became something of an expert in taking care of Keli. She always felt secure, loved, and entertained, even though it was completely exhausting. When something bothered her, we found a solution to make it easier for her. Sometimes these were of my own creation but often I consulted the experts. I hope that my experiences and research will save you and your little one a lot of heartache and time. I will never know why Keli had colic, food allergies, and sensitivity. I suspect there is

some relationship between them. Eventually, I decided that understanding the causes was less important than learning the solutions and I began to focus on just that: the solutions.

Due to her personality and food allergies, we've had many challenges (and still do) while raising our daughter, who is now three. Maybe this introduction lacks a big bang kind of ending where I talk about the worst day of my life or how our family fell apart as a result of all of this, but if you're in the shoes now that we wore then, you already know that there is no big bang. Taking care of your first child is the most trying thing you will eve do. Your patience, perseverance, and perception of self will all be challenged. You will gain a new understanding of your capacity for selflessness, which will amaze you. All children are a lot of hard work and all Attachment Parents are heroes.

CHAPTER 1:
Early Days

Babywearing

Babywearing is said to contribute to a strong emotional bond between you and your child, and it is a key feature of Attachment Parenting. Babywearing is practiced when you carry your child in a baby carrier (sling, wrap, or other) on your front, hip, or back. Such carriers often replace bouncy chairs and swings in your home or strollers when you are out. As a new Attachment Parent, you're already committed to the idea of babywearing. You've started researching carriers but still have questions. You haven't the faintest idea what all the hoopla on the Internet is regarding designer wraps, and the term "crotch dangler" is somewhat, though not as much as you would like it to be, obscure to you. You're not sure which carrier to buy but you're thinking that you'll try to avoid those two-hundred-dollar carriers because your baby won't know the difference.

When your baby is 0-3-months-old, it is best to use a wrap-style carrier. Your baby will enjoy being held closely against your heartbeat.

On the flipside, you're someone who knows exactly what carrier you'll buy because it's gorgeous, so why wouldn't your little one love it? You probably think that your baby is going to love being carried around while you get on with life-before-baby, as you knew it.

I want to suggest humbly that you can't prepare for babywearing; you won't know what it's like until you've experienced it. Babywearing is a relationship between you, your child, and a piece of cloth, and it will present new challenges along the way.

There are three main considerations when preparing to babywear:

Type of carrier and how to wear it

It's not possible to give how-to instructions on all of the different types of carrier, but you'll find fantastic videos and tutorials on how to use any carrier that you purchase on the Internet. The type of carrier you choose will depend on the age, size, and preference of your child; there is no perfect answer, but here are some guidelines that I've found represent what works for many parents.

Birth to 3 months (wrap): At this time your little one is very small and will most likely enjoy the womb-like effect of being on your front, close and snug against your heartbeat and warmth.

3 months to 6 months (outward-facing carry): These are most commonly designed in the narrow base carrier or "crotch-dangling" style (the baby's weight is mainly held by fabric between the legs, rather than a more supportive style that cradles and supports the bottom), but you can find some that are more supportive than others. Around this time, he may begin to resist the constrictive sling and become peaceful and happy only when walking around with you, observing his surroundings, and

taking things in. Facing outward is a good position because your baby is becoming aware of his external environment; however, I would recommend using this carry style only on occasion to minimize any discomfort to your child's hips and legs.

6 months to 1 year (child facing inward in the support of a square panel): You would think that the above would still be true, that your child wants to be able to observe his environment, but the crotch-dangler carriers are uncomfortable and become more so with the increasing weight of the baby. Your six-month-old child will be large enough to turn his

From 6 months to 1 year, an inward-facing carry in a structured carrier is the best option for your child.

head to look behind him and so will still have visibility. If your child begins to resist the narrow-base carrier or never gets to like it, skip straight to the latter style. Since this style is designed for babies who weigh at least sixteen pounds, it's usually too deep for a smaller baby to sit in while having good visibility. A tip for this is to roll up a baby blanket and line the bottom of the carrier, making a raised seat for your little one. Then he'll be three or four inches higher. This worked wonders for us. Also, a younger baby may not have long enough legs for this type of carrier, causing unnatural spreading. The rolled-up blanket also solves this problem: when your child sits on it he will be elevated, therefore his legs will have ample room without having to be spread (almost as if he were sitting on a chair inside of the carrier.)

1 year on (same as above): Most parents keep using the carrier described above but start wearing their child on their back. There won't be any need for a lot of guessing at this point. Your child will tell you if he's uncomfortable.

What to do when your little one resists being worn

If your child is resisting being worn, first consider the issue of comfort. I had questions about where Keli's legs and head should be when being carried. You'll notice when you first begin babywearing that some of the positions seem unnatural and look rather uncomfortable. Some moms are pretty easygoing about this, not minding if their baby's head is covered up or his legs are spread wide or squished up. I was persistent about finding the right position because otherwise Keli would resist being worn.

Some common discomforts children experience while being worn include feeling too constricted in wraps, the discomfort that comes with unequal

When your child is one year or older, you will likely start to carry them on your back and your child will be able to tell you if they are experiencing any discomfort.

weight distribution in narrow-base carriers; and the obstruction to vision that some carriers cause. Try your best to tune in to what it is that your baby is resisting and then experiment with different tricks and adjustments to ease these discomforts.

Finally, try not to be tricked into thinking something is wrong with the carrier you're using at the moment simply because nothing you try seems to be working. Give your baby time to get used to a new carrier: begin walking him around in it even if he is crying; he may surprise you and stop.

How to avoid babywearing expenses

Try not to dismiss the idea of purchasing a more expensive carrier if you're confident it is a good one. If you can get a good deal on a nice carrier, that's great, but if you find that less expensive carriers are not working for you, it may very well be the quality of it rather than the style.

Mistakes and misconceptions

Babywearing mamas can be rather passionate about their practice. Many groups dedicated specifically to babywearing meet regularly. Aside from socializing and sharing a love of babywearing, there is another important reason for these meetings: the difficulty of babywearing. Babywearing can be expensive and impractical and, if taken for granted as being natural and efficient, it can be disappointing.

When I attended babywearing groups, I received carrier recommendations and learned new carrying techniques; the most useful advice I received, however, was often about what not to do rather than what to do. It was helpful to hear what other mothers would do differently if they could start over.

 HELPFUL HINTS

With so much in the way of experimenting, how can one avoid the high expenses of baby carrying?

1 Make your own sling.

2 Avoid designer-wrap frenzy (or the impulse to have a collection of carriers.)

3 If you know babywearing moms, ask them if you can borrow one of their carriers before purchasing one for yourself. They probably have one or two that are not being used at the moment. If you don't have babywearing friends, think about joining a local babywearing group.

4 There's no shame in buying one, holding onto the receipt, and returning it soon after if you are sure it's not right for your baby.

5 Hold a carrier swap. This is where you invite your babywearing friends to a party and ask them to bring their no-longer-loved carriers. The idea here is that you can put yours in a pile and take a new one out.

Five Mistakes I Made With Babywearing

1 **I was over-confident.** Do either of these thoughts sound familiar? "I'll just carry her and my life will go on as normal." "We don't need to go home for naps; she'll nap on my back when I go grocery shopping." If so, keep in mind that while it's good to be positive, it's equally important to be realistic. I would babywear again but I became frustrated with it many times. My overall experience would have been better if I hadn't gone into it with so many expectations and assumptions.

2 **I naively thought that I would simply strap Keli onto my chest and get on with dinner.** When I was wearing Keli on my front (the only way she liked to be worn,) I couldn't reach my arms out in front of me in such a way as to be able do anything. The few times I tried awkwardly to do something with her on my front, I couldn't see my hands or what I was holding. If you can wear your child on your back, however, you might get some work done but many AP mothers I know are only comfortable with back wearing when their child is older.

3 **I thought that all babies love to be worn.** Before Keli was six months old, she didn't enjoy being worn much at all. Once she was six months old, she was only content to be worn if we were on an outing or if it was naptime. If I could do it all over again, I would not see strollers as the enemy. Keli weighed twenty pounds by the time she was four months old. I loved holding her, but when she became heavy for me it was difficult to go anywhere with her as my arms often became tired.

4 **I worried too much.** No matter which carrier you choose in the beginning, it is likely to devour your tiny baby. I was uncomfortable not being able to see Keli's face. As I didn't want to feel anxious, and in turn have Keli sense that there was something negative about being worn, I had a tendency to wear her in ways that were a physical strain on me. I should have spoken to more mothers about this fear and worked to come up with something that was safe but also enjoyable for me.

5 **I thought babywearing was a great way to nap my baby.** It is normal for babies to start resisting sleep times as they develop and become more engrossed in learning about their surroundings, and I thought that babywearing would encourage her to sleep. In reality, pacing around the house for ninety minutes with a twenty-six-pound baby was not all I had dreamed of. I had more luck getting Keli to nap off me when the carrier was not involved. I never actually transferred her successfully from carrier to bed without waking her. What's more, she'd wake up even if I sat down. To most people, this might sound like torture. To the Attachment Parent, it's routine. I should have taken her out of the carrier right before she fell asleep and then nursed her down or carried her in my arms until she was asleep so that I could be freed from nap-enslavement.

Your Colicky Baby

If you have a colicky baby, it can sometimes feel like there's a hex on your child. This might sound dramatic, but many parents who have been awake in the small hours of the morning with a colicky child will agree that it's no exaggeration!

Fortunately, there is no hex on your child; your child "has" colic. I've used quotation marks because colic is not something a baby has, at least not in the way we usually think. You have a cold, not a runny nose. You have an ear infection, not a sore ear. The runny nose and the sore ear are symptoms; the cold and the ear infection are the diagnoses. There are a few medical examples where the diagnoses and the symptoms are identically labeled, as with colic. This can happen when doctors don't understand the underlying roots of a set of frequently recurring symptoms that are assumed to have a medical cause.

Understanding colic

If you're like me, when your friends or doctor tell you that it sounds like your child has colic, you'll go home and begin to research it. The exact list of symptoms that you already know she has comes up again and again under the term colic. You can now say, "My child has colic," but soon after feeling this relief, you'll feel let down when you discover that there is absolutely no indication as to what causes it or how to treat it. In my opinion, this is not a true diagnosis.

What was causing my child's colic? Or, as I prefer to phrase it nowadays: what did she have rather than colic? I began to think she was teething early. I ruled it out. It was true that she was chewing on my shoulders and biting on her hands, but I now know that she was biting on my shoulder as a way of bearing the pain she was feeling. It was easy to rule out other culprits such as fever, cold, ear infection, broken toe, and diaper rash because these have other obvious symptoms. This led me to believe that the cause of her colic must be invisible.

When I spoke to Keli's pediatrician, he suggested that severe gas pains can cause it. This is a reasonable guess but one problem with using gas to explain colic is that there is nothing a parent can do to eliminate gas completely. I ruled out gas, believing that gas pains could not send my daughter into hysterical screaming fits for hours on end. But there did seem to be something behind the idea, and I continued my research. Gastroenterologist, Dr. Bryan Vartabedian, wrote the book *Colic Solved: The Essential Guide to*

Infant Reflux and the Care of Your Crying, Difficult-to-Soothe Baby. In his book, Vartabedian explains that your child's digestive system may respond negatively to her diet, which may be the cause of colic. Many cases of colic have been discovered to be reflux or other forms of gastrointestinal intolerances. Reflux, milk protein allergies, protein induced proctitis, and GERD (gastroesophageal reflux disease) can all be the cause of colic. According to Vartabedian, there is a high correlation between colic and digestive problems in babies, and it is possible that there is more than one condition present. For instance, antibiotics in a newborn can cause leaky-gut syndrome, which in turn can cause food allergies. The food allergies may then cause reflux or GERD.

Colic and food allergies

There are many foods that parents know should be avoided until their baby is six months of age; this helps to prevent food allergies (cow's milk, soy, wheat, peanuts, corn, and eggs.) If you think about it, breast-feeding babies are exposed to all of the proteins in these foods via their mother's milk from birth, so even if it seems unlikely that your child can be reacting to your milk, it's quite possible that she is reacting to your diet.

At two months old, Keli's reflux became visible (she started projectile vomiting) and she became extremely agitated. I realized that the amount of wheat and cow's milk in my diet had increased and I wondered if this could be linked to Keli's reflux. I researched possible causes of reflux and, sure enough, food allergies were listed. As soon as I discovered that she had reflux, I knew that this had been the cause of her colic. Her pediatrician confirmed that she was suffering from acid reflux and prescribed a medication. We discovered that what many mothers report was also true for us—that the reflux medication given to us by the pediatrician did not do anything to cure our child's reflux. My husband was reluctant to follow our doctor's suggestions to increase her dose or give her stronger forms of this medicine because acid-blocking drugs cause changes in the internal environment of the stomach that can lead to ongoing health problems.

I was happy to have some answers, but it wasn't until I read that food allergies could be the cause of her reflux that I felt that I was on the right track. I began Dr. Sears' elimination diet and within three weeks Keli's colic was gone. Of course, all babies are different and what was true for my daughter might not be true for your child. However, I strongly recommend Dr. Vartabedian's book to anyone struggling with a colicky child.

HELPFUL HINTS

Below are some general tips for helping a colicky baby:

1 **Try changing your baby's formula** to a dairy and soy-free based formula.

2 **Eliminate common allergy-causing foods** from the breast-feeding mother's diet.

3 **Give your baby probiotics**, especially if he's on antibiotics. Dr. Vartabedian explains that giving colicky babies probiotics can reduce crying by as much as 50 percent (check with your pediatrician about dose, brands, and safety.)

4 **Be careful not to overfeed** your baby.

5 **Make sure to burp your baby** frequently.

6 **If you have a heavy milk flow, implement block feeding.** This is when you feed your child on one breast per feeding, rather than switching to the other breast. At first, when the baby latches on, he receives foremilk and then, after a little while, hindmilk, which is thicker and easier on the stomach. If you have an oversupply of milk, switching to the other breast can result in too much foremilk. Block feeding will help to slow the flow so that

your child will not swallow as much air and will also ensure that he is not drinking too much foremilk. Both of these problems are common with heavy milk flows and can irritate the stomach. Block feeding may also send a message to your body that less milk is needed, and so the supply will drop.

7 **If you bottle-feed** switch to a bottle that keeps babies from swallowing excess air.

8 **Lay your child on his back,** hold each of his calves in one of your hands, and slowly push his knees to his belly button. Gas may not be the only problem your colicky child has but it is likely present with any digestive problem he may be experiencing. This will bring some relief.

9 **If your child has reflux** or if you suspect acid reflux that is not always visible, talk to a pediatrician about giving him a small dose of Mylanta or Mylicon.

10 **Trust your intuition.** If you think your child is in pain, don't give up on finding the cause and treatment that he needs.

Your High-Need Baby

Mistaken about the facts, some people believe that Attachment Parenting causes high-need behavior. However, people who have high-need babies know that their child's high need is the main reason they become Attachment Parents! Dr. Sears who, as already discussed, created the term "Attachment Parenting," explains, without ambiguity, that the development of this parenting style was a direct response to learning how to take care of Hayden, his fourth-born child and his first high-need baby.

Recognizing the signs

Some children are not relaxed and easygoing, cannot be trained to adjust to things, and don't fall into a routine with the right amount of practice; they won't be held by others and have emotional meltdowns instead of crying fits. If you're nodding your head to any of this, you might have a high-need baby—and even if you did not plan to practice Attachment Parenting with your newborn, the fact that she classifies as a high-need baby means that some form of attachment parenting is bound to follow.

High-need babies can also be recognized by their exceptional clinginess, constant crying, and easy waking. They are known for cries that quickly escalate into fits of screaming hysteria that are almost impossible to calm. It becomes necessary, for your newborn's happiness as well as your own, to sleep near your child, carry him all day, and attend to his crying as quickly as possible, all of which are very much AP practices. High-need babies are not happy sleeping alone in a crib, being set down in a bouncy chair, sitting in a car seat, or being left with anyone while mommy goes out for an hour. When the parent of a high-need baby sees another baby sitting quietly out of its mother's arms, they feel disbelief that it's possible. Put simply, high-need babies need more of their parents' attention.

My daughter Keli was a high-need baby. She fell under all twelve of Dr. Sears' high-need baby features, as listed in *The Baby Book*. Anyone who has a high-need baby knows that it's an around-the-clock job. At the end of each day, my only positive feeling was the one that stemmed from knowing that my husband and I were doing all we could to make our child happy. Fortunately, I had already intended to practice Attachment Parenting, but because of that my friends often insinuated that if I simply let Keli cry more often, she wouldn't expect to be held all of the time and nursed to sleep. What they didn't know is that Keli would have become worse very quickly had I followed their advice. What people don't understand about high-need babies is that they are not just demanding; they are in the truest sense more needy and sensitive than other babies.

The twelve signs of a high-need baby, as listed in *The Baby Book*, are as follows. Keep in mind that all babies exhibit these traits sometimes. A high-need baby exhibits many of these traits most of the time.

* Intense
* Hyperactive
* Draining
* Feeds frequently
* Demanding
* Awakens frequently
* Unsatisfied
* Unpredictable
* Hypersensitive
* Needs to be held constantly
* Not a self-soother
* Separation-sensitive

I admit that our gentle parenting style with Keli has resulted largely in an unrestricted environment that makes for behaviors that could just as easily be seen as the result of a spoiled rather than a high-need child. However, we created this environment based on Keli's needs rather than creating such an environment in advance only to see her personality change accordingly. Due to the feeling of security that Attachment Parenting provides, high-need children will outgrow many of these trying traits more quickly than if left on their own to learn coping mechanisms. Once a high-need baby's needs are met, he will flourish, becoming happier and easier right before your eyes.

Finding solutions

When your child is able to understand and communicate more, it's important to work on changing clingy and demanding behavior. Once he is old enough to talk with you, focus on finding solutions together and discouraging negative behaviors. Keli is now a highly-sensitive toddler, requiring a lot of attention that demands a completely different set of management tools. Some of the tips below may work for toddlers, but please see the highly-sensitive toddler section in chapter 5 if your child is older.

❋ HELPFUL HINTS

1 Surrender. The sooner you stop resisting, the happier you will be. There will be phases of intense dependency. Sometimes these phases come when you thought you were over the worst of it. Remember that it's just a phase and that it will pass more quickly when your little one gets the attention and holding that she needs. Responding to your baby's needs is a form of physical surrender, but of equal importance is the emotional surrender that can be accomplished by sympathizing with your child even at trying moments.

2 Consider possible stressors and make changes accordingly. Ask yourself the following questions and make any necessary changes: Is she getting enough sleep? Seeing enough of both caregivers? Has she had any big changes in her life recently? Is she spending enough time at home, getting out to recharge? Is she in an over-stimulating situation? Is she getting enough quiet time with her primary caregiver? Is she ill or teething?

3 Always have a back-up plan. High-need babies often don't make it to the end of whatever you have planned for them. If you are planning an outing, be aware that you may need to head home early. Before you leave, pack the necessary things for her comfort and pick quiet places where you will be able to help her re-gather if need be.

4 Don't expect people to understand that your child is high need. If you speak to others looking for advice about your high-need child, they will most often give advice that applies to a non-high-need child. Try not to second-guess yourself if you're pretty sure that the advice you're being given will not sit well with your high-need baby.

5 Stay home. Of course you won't stay home all of the time, but if you have a high-need child you may notice that staying home is better for her than going out (especially in the early days.) At home you can nurse, cuddle, and walk your baby to her heart's content. You can ignore your phone and emails while spending the entire afternoon playing with your child on the floor. However, don't let this be your routine: keep trying new situations with your little one. One day she will be better at handling a situation that previously would have been overwhelming.

6 Pack distractions. When going out, pack several things that can be used as distractions. Some of the situations that have upset Keli when we were out include too many people, me talking to someone (even when I was wearing her,) sitting in the car seat, the weather, and loud sounds. I use the word "meltdown" to explain when a high-need child is so worked up that it can take an hour to calm her down. Bring her snacks, new or favorite toys, juice, or something she always wants but you never let her have in those pre-meltdown moments. This will be a sure distraction, buying you just enough time to change the situation. I recommend that you come up with a new plan while your child is happy; otherwise, once the distraction stops working, she will likely become worked up again.

7 Adjust your schedules. This is not an easy one, but if at all possible for both you and your partner, adjust your work schedules so that you're both home together more often. One person taking care of a high-need baby is draining to say the least. This is a two-person job, so if you can afford a pay cut, I suggest reducing your hours at work and spending those gained in the house. Looking after your little one is two full-time jobs, and both you and your partner will need to be on board at all possible times.

8 Get support. If the previous suggestion is not possible, come up with a system that guarantees both of you baby-free breaks (preferably out of the house). It always helped me to know when my next break was coming. We stayed aware of who had Keli for long stretches and found an overall balance of responsibilities so that no one had her all of the time. Your child will probably not do well with a babysitter, but if you are considering going that route, choose someone familiar and introduce the situation over a long period of time. Be on hand for the first few babysitting days in case it's not working out. If you are right there

when your baby really needs you (you'll know those cries,) then her anxiety about being left with other people will most likely ease up.

9 Educate and stimulate. High-need babies tend to have advanced intelligence. Don't hesitate to teach them at a more advanced level than other children their age. If your high-need child is surrounded by educational toys and has you to engage with, it will add to her overall happiness and lighten her disposition. Start with language and eventually move forward (see education section, pages 130–137.) Not only will she enjoy the attention, but she will also be receiving some of the necessary tools to communicate. The sooner communication is available to a high-need child, the easier life becomes for both of you.

10 Remember soothing tricks. It will seem like your little one cannot self-soothe, ever, and you'll need more than just one trick up your sleeve for the various situations that will upset her. Learn a few techniques for helping your baby sleep and how to keep her happy in the car if you have to travel. For instance, I always sat in the back seat with my daughter and hardly drove anywhere without my husband for months. Some tricks will require more work and sacrifice than others, but if they work, stick with them. Learn songs that she likes, games that always cheer her up, distractions that work, and diaper-changing and getting-dressed tricks.

Moving House or Going on Vacation with Your Baby

It's natural for parents to feel nervous about their first trip away from home with a new baby or even a toddler if that's how long it's been since the family had a vacation. Attachment Parents might feel more anxious because, generally speaking, their children are less accustomed to sharing their parents, which may be difficult to avoid on vacation. Then there's moving house, which is inexplicably more stressful. The nature of the fears can vary: Will our child adjust to her new surroundings? Will our daughter's sleep schedule be affected? Will she continue to eat on schedule or will we see behavior changes in her? I would be lying if I told you there was no reason to have such concerns. Some children adjust to change quickly, some take much longer, but most will be affected in some way.

We found that with the right amount of preparation and attention, we didn't need to worry that our daughter would be traumatized in those first weeks. We have flown five times since Keli was born and moved into a new home three times, so, in the circumstances, I'm inclined to think that we are as expert in this field as any parent. I've collected and practiced good tips along the way that have made our experiences much easier on Keli and on us, and they may in turn help you. This section is about settling into a new environment (be it permanent or on vacation) with your little one.

❋ HELPFUL HINTS

1 **If you're moving, pack gradually so that the house doesn't suddenly feel empty.** We left all of the big stuff (furniture and play areas) for the very last day, and in fact Keli never saw the house fully empty because I had her in the new place with a play area set up while the movers did the rest. Having her toys in her new home meant she could have fun, and although it was bare, she didn't mind because she'd never seen it any other way. The rest of the stuff arrived an hour later. Alternatively, you could pack everything in one day while your partner takes your child out, and then you take over childcare when it's time to help the movers. The important thing is that your little one never sees either house completely empty and is not stuck inside all day watching her things come down around her.

2 **After moving into a new home, take your child outside often during the first two weeks.** Our daughter did fine for about two days but as the novelty wore off, I noticed that she was more aimless in her mood than she had been at the previous place. She'd been queen of her world in the old house and now she seemed out of her element. During this time I took her out a lot so that she wouldn't have a chance to miss the old house. If she seemed anxious or aimless, I would hurry her out before she became sad. This seemed to ease the transition and a few weeks later she was queen of the new place, too.

3 **Avoid showing pictures or videos of the old residence.** We like to look at old photos with Keli. She enjoys seeing baby pictures and hearing stories, but I didn't do this for several months after we moved into the new place. It could have been confusing or made her miss something she'd mostly forgotten about. After some time you don't have to worry about it, but it's a good idea to be cautious about looking at old photos or videos together in the beginning.

4 **Keep things that are key to your child's environment.** Even if you no longer need the six-foot by six-foot fluorescent floor mat, keep it. This is the sort of thing your child will notice is missing. No matter what your end plan for your new place is, try to keep it looking very similar to the old one in the beginning, in particular her sleeping area. Make it a close replica of the one she previously slept in.

5 **Don't suddenly change the nighttime routine.** Whether moving or vacationing, be careful not to change elements such as lighting, position of the bed in the room, having a noise machine, and routines such as brushing teeth followed by putting on pajamas, etc. Make sure all of the sleep aides you use are unpacked for that very first nap and bedtime in the new house. Be sure to be in the room when your child wakes up the first few or, if necessary, many times in the new place because she is likely to feel disoriented, confused, and alone waking up somewhere new.

7 **Make sure to have your child's favorite foods around.** When we travel, the food available might be very different from what we're used to, or we can be too busy to consider food and end up with quite a different diet. Your child, however, will appreciate consistency in this regard. When I say appreciate it, I mean she might go hungry if you don't, so a bit of forward planning is necessary. Be sure to pack her accustomed foods, buy them when you get there, or have your host pick them up before you arrive.

8 **Pack all your child's favorite things.** Of course you wouldn't leave your child's favorite things behind when moving, so this advice applies more so to vacationing. In terms of moving, I would like to add that it's a good idea to unpack her favorite things first. This could include favorite books, CDs, night-lights, pillows, toys, and stuffed animals; think about cups, spoons, toys, and puzzles that she is especially fond of. There will come a time on your vacation when your little one wants to be at home. If you have a corner of your hotel room or friend's house set up with these things, she will feel better during such moments.

6 **Spend quality time with your little one.** You will be very busy when you've just moved or arrived on vacation and it will be tempting to try to get your child to entertain herself, but she will adjust better to change if you are present with her. You'll likely feel stressed out and feeling present mentally, as well as physically, at the same time will be a challenge, but one that is well worth the outcome. Talk about the new situation, make sure that your little one is having fun and feeling secure in her new environment. If she begins to feel homesick, take her for a quiet walk alone so that you can help her to feel grounded again.

9 **Communicate with others ahead of time.** Make sure your host knows what your child's needs are. I'm not just referring to food, bedding, and lighting, but also to the length of her bedtime routine, what types of situation (e.g. car seats, loud dogs, high-pitched laughing) make her feel fussed. You can't avoid these situations but if this is all clear from the start, you won't feel rushed, pulled in two directions, or anxious when something causes upset. This tip also works for moving. Talk to your partner about when you'll both take breaks to have family time, discuss situations that should be avoided (e.g. hanging pictures while the baby is home,) and make sure you're both committed to keeping your child's schedule the same regardless of what is going on around you.

10 **Communicate with your child ahead of time.** Whether you are moving or vacationing, it's important to let your child know what to expect in the coming days. Go a step beyond this and highlight the exciting parts so that she looks forward to the adventure. Spend time talking about aspects of the move or trip that you assume will be hard for her. Sometimes we get so busy that we forget that our little ones are as much a part of this process as we are. Don't underestimate the benefits of a heart-to-heart with your child, even if she is only two years old. If you're moving, I recommend reading *The Berenstain's Bears Moving Day* by Stan Berenstain together.

CHAPTER 2:
Sleep

Co-sleeping

My husband asked a daddy friend of his, "If you could give me a single piece of advice about parenting, what would it be?" His friend responded, "Let your child sleep in your bed." We had already decided to co-sleep but it wasn't until his friend said this that I wondered about the glorious benefits of co-sleeping. Why was this the best piece of advice he could give us?

I had decided to co-sleep with Keli because I knew I'd be breast-feeding her and the idea of waking up in the middle of the night, walking over to her crib, nursing her, and trying to put her down when I was absolutely exhausted seemed like a miserable one. A little bit of babysitting experience had taught me well that cribs and babies are not good friends. I'm a "pick-your-battles" type of mama and I knew long before having Keli that this was a battle I'd never know.

I also decided to co-sleep based on a commitment I made at the very beginning of our pregnancy to keep things simple. We wouldn't buy tons of clothes, bottles, fancy forks, or nursery decals. We wouldn't purchase fancy strollers, newborn dress shoes, and fruit that squeezes out of a pouch. Co-sleeping seemed to fit with my simple intentions for parenting. I read up on the safety tips and committed to co-sleeping.

Five benefits of co-sleeping

✳ More snuggles
✳ Less Worry
✳ Less getting up from bed
✳ Easier time getting her to sleep and stay asleep
✳ Simplicity

If it were that simple, then everyone would do co-sleeping. But it's not all simple—yet another AP practice that turns out to be complicated. It's worth considering the following points and thinking about the balance between the sacrifices made and the benefits gained. Think about safety, how well you and your child will sleep in close proximity to each other, the transition from husband-and-wife bed to family bed, and, finally, the challenges you will experience when moving your child to her own bedroom.

My instincts told me that co-sleeping was safer than putting Keli in a crib and everything other than safety seemed a minor concern. There wasn't much I wouldn't have endured to ensure that my husband, Keli, and I slept well for the first year of her life. And although we didn't know it then, for the second and third years of her life, too.

In deciding what I wanted to write about for this section, I asked myself, "What are the most challenging aspects of co-sleeping?" My brain flashbacked to the co-sleeping conversations that took place at the mommy forums I frequented. There were generally two concerns, the first being safety and the second how to co-sleep.

"Getting started"

When we first began co-sleeping, it was an awkward experience. I wasn't sure how to keep myself warm while keeping the blanket completely away from Keli's face. One assumes that using a pillow is easy, but when you're co-sleeping with a newborn, you begin to wonder why your pillow didn't come with an instruction manual. I didn't know how to dress my daughter for bedtime. If she couldn't be under the blankets, I knew I should dress her warmly, but babies sleep better if they are a bit too cool rather than a little too warm. My husband and I had long,

At 0-3 months, your child will be sleeping on his back, about twelve inches away from you. If you have a blanket, wrap yourself tightly so that it won't come loose. Make sure that your pillow is kept away from your baby.

analytical debates about our pajama choices for our daughter.

As Keli began to crawl and roam around on the bed, new challenges arose. I needed to learn how to leave her in our family bed for naptime so that I could get things done while being certain that she wouldn't fall off the bed. Such considerations became necessary at nighttime too. When she became a toddler, we had more problems—"she's in my way, she's still nursing throughout the night, maybe I need to move away from her, and maybe she'd sleep better if she had her own space... It sure would be nice to have my husband back in bed."

The following is a glimpse at how I successfully co-slept and how my techniques changed as my baby went from newborn to toddler. I hope that this section will be useful and helpful, but please keep in mind that this is my experience and what worked for me; it won't necessarily work for all co-sleepers. Please be aware of and follow the co-sleeping safety guidelines at all times.

Newborn to three months old

Your child's position in bed: Your child should sleep on her back until she is able to roll over on her own. Before that time, she won't fall off the bed if you keep her on the outside of you. That is to say, with a bird's eye view of the bed, your partner is on the left of you, you are in the middle and your child is on the right of you. This keeps your baby safe from being sandwiched between you and your partnerk. It also keeps her away from dad, who is likely to be less aware of a sleeping baby than mom.

Position of the bed: At this point, it doesn't matter where your bed is or how you've set it up for safety. Your child isn't moving around so you can have your bed anywhere in the room, without rails or pillows on the floor. Remember to keep a tight sheet on the bed and make sure that your mattress is firm.

Bedding: If you want to use a blanket for yourself, use a small one. Your partner should probably have his own because you're going to need more freedom now that you're waking to nurse your baby. Wrap yourself, starting under your arms, tuck it under your body so that it's not loose and won't fall near your baby. If you want to use a pillow, be sure that it is not close to your baby. You don't want to have your child's and your head at the same level if you're using a pillow because that would mean that she is much too close to the pillow. Whenever you wake to nurse would be a good time to check that the blanket, pillow, and baby have not shifted. If you live in a cold climate, you could give your baby a light muslin sheet for warmth.

Your position: I kept Keli about twelve inches away from me when I was sleeping. I found that when she was closer than this to me, she or I would somehow wiggle a little closer until we were too close for comfort. If your baby wants to nurse, you're going to find this a bit uncomfortable as you won't know what to do with your arms. I recommend putting one arm under your pillow (bent as if you were going to lay on it as a pillow) and resting the other on your hip.

It's important not to fall asleep while nursing your baby. If you doubt your ability to do this, sit up for night wakings. This will make it more difficult for you both to resettle, but it is extremely dangerous to fall asleep while nursing a newborn in bed. If you don't

trust yourself to remember this, and you think you might sleepily nurse your child, wear a restrictive bra or something that would require full waking in order to nurse. When she is done nursing, move her back to where she was or move away from your baby. I would move away from Keli so as not to wake her.

Three months old to crawling

Your child's position in bed: If your child is not turning over, she should still be sleeping on her back. I would add that even though your little one may not be rolling over yet, she may be capable of it. For this reason, once Keli was of rolling age, she slept between my husband and I. If you are still not comfortable with your partner sleeping near your baby, think about changing the position of your bed.

Position of the bed: You might move the bed against a wall so that your child sleeps between you and the wall. You can also look into attaching a bed railing on one side of the bed. There are different types available, and if you or someone you know has carpentry skills, you could even have a railing made. Some people use an oversized swim noodle tucked tightly under the sheet to create a railing. Despite my strong desire to leave my bedroom aesthetically pleasing, we chose to move the bed against a wall. My daughter wasn't crawling, so I didn't have to worry too much about the foot of the bed, but I put extra blankets on the floor there just in case she fell.

At naptime, I would leave the door open and keep an eye on her. I believed it unlikely that she'd manage to roll to the edge of the bed, especially if I

Crawling to 1 year: Moving your mattress onto the floor is the safest thing to do once your baby starts to crawl. Line the floor with blankets to avoid any bruises should your child crawl off the mattress.

was regularly peeking in at her to see if she was nearing the edge. However, to be extra safe, I lined the whole floor around the bed with blankets. This was nerve-wracking for me and I moved on to the bed position discussed in the next stage rather quickly.

Bedding: All the advice given in the previous stage still applies. Your little one may be sleeping on her stomach. If so, it is wise to check her nose and mouth and make sure that the bed surface is not so soft that it blocks these openings and her ability to breathe. Do this every night because it may be that your sheet needs to be tucked tighter or your bed has become softer since you first bought it. By now your little one should be able to wake and move herself if she is not getting air, but you can't be too

careful. Some parents might want to give their child a blanket at this stage, but it could become tangled and restricting beyond a young baby's ability to free herself. If you're ready to give your baby a blanket, make sure it's a small one.

Your position: To be as safe as possible, you should remain in the same position that you were in when your baby was a newborn. Some people say that once your child can roll over and move away from you or a pillow, you do not need to worry as much about suffocation hazards. However, I wasn't comfortable with this idea and preferred to be as safe as I possibly could.

Crawling to one year old

Your child's position in bed: You're not really in control of her position any longer. Crawling gives your baby full freedom. By now you probably are not worried about her sleeping next to your partner. Your child can and will sleep anywhere in the bed and this includes on top of you, under your neck, and right smack in the middle of the bed.

Position of the bed: Despite saying to yourself, "I will not put my mattress on the floor, I will not put my mattress on the floor, I will not put my mattress on the floor," you are probably going to put your mattress on the floor. Why? Because it's the safest thing you can do when you have a crawling baby sleeping in your bed. Just how mobile your child is will help you decide when to do this. Once your child is crawling, her ability to get near the edge of the bed trumps your ability to keep a close eye on her. It'll happen fast, if it happens. When the mattress is on the floor, you can put your child between you and your partner at bedtime. Line the floor at the bottom of the bed with blankets. This would be a small and harmless fall, of course, but just to avoid any unnecessary bruises and tears in the night, it's a good precaution to take. I didn't want to worry about Keli during her nap, so I found it most sensible to have the mattress against one wall and have blankets all around it. I might have tried the swim noodle trick at this point, but I didn't know about it then.

Bedding: The tips I described in the above stages still apply. By now I was giving Keli her own blanket.

Your position: Now that your child has head control and can move away from you on her own, you can try some new things to help you get comfortable. The pillow should still stay away from your baby whenever possible. Some parents will be giving their child their own baby pillow by now. I didn't give Keli a pillow, but because she was quite mobile in our co-sleeping bed, it wasn't easy to keep her away from my pillow at all times. If you feel uneasy about this, remove the pillow.

As your child gets bigger, it's hard to nurse her while keeping her far away from your pillow. My tall one-year-old took up too much space for that position. Instead, to nurse her, I would move the pillow. She and I could then use my bent arm as pillow so that she could reach the breast. As soon as she fell asleep, I'd move away from her and use my pillow again. Try not to get trapped into an awkward position.

One year old to toddler

Your child's position in bed: The same as stated in the previous stage applies here. Although I found it perfectly safe for Keli to sleep between my husband and myself, I tried to keep her between me and the wall only because my husband's stirring woke her.

Position of the bed: Most of what I said in the previous stage remained true for us. Based on advice I had read suggesting that my toddler might wake less at night if she had her own space, I introduced a co-sleeper to the bed. When I say co-sleeper, I mean a crib with one side down. We were gifted a crib that converted into a toddler bed so this piece was designed to be removed. In order to make it perfectly level with my bed I had to put the mattress back on its frame. Not surprisingly, I had to trick Keli to go for it. I would lie close enough to her and nurse her while she was in her own bed so that she didn't even notice that they were two separate beds. While it was great that she fell asleep in her own bed, I couldn't sleep like this because it was terribly uncomfortable. I would go back to my spot feeling triumphant only to have an awakened toddler find her way to me an hour later. If your toddler needs and wants more space, then do give it a try. Keli didn't need or want more space. She wanted mommy and I chose not to fight this battle. If there are three or more of you in a bed and you don't have a king-sized mattress, I recommend getting one.

Bedding: It seems as though anything goes at this point. Just remember that if your child is getting a blanket and pillow now, they should be the appropriate size.

Your position: This seems like a good time to mention that you can now do all of the snuggling you want. I believe all positioning to be fair game at this point. At this age, your child will wake you up if you are in her way. And just to follow through with the advice I picked up about toddlers needing more space, I'd move to the other side of the bed once Keli was asleep. This also seemed to prevent her from nursing as much.

Sleep Plan

We didn't have a sleep routine or plan for the first year of Keli's life. It was okay with us if she went to bed and slept in later than most babies. Most of the time she managed to sleep twelve hours, so we felt at peace with her schedule. Then came the fighting-sleep era (at just over a year old.) The problem with this is that although her bedtime changed, her wake-up time did not. Her twelve hours became nine, and it was evident in her mood the next day. I knew that I needed to get stricter about when she went to bed. According to the experts, earlier is better. The fighting was frequent and intense because we were letting her stay up too late, so I began to put her down earlier but she only reacted by fighting for longer. A vicious cycle began that lasted for around eight weeks.

Sleep assessment

At times like these it can seem as though you don't have any control over your child's sleeping habits, but in fact you can maintain a great amount of control by creating a sleep plan. The following two steps will help you to put it together. First, complete something that I call a sleep assessment. Oftentimes, exhausted parents haven't honed in on the changes they would like to see in their child's sleep. All they know is that something isn't working. If you don't have a clear image in your mind about what you'd like to see in terms of your child's sleep habits, consistency will be near impossible to develop. Once this assessment is complete, goals will naturally emerge, as will the areas you need to focus on for change. Write down answers to the following questions:

* How long is my child sleeping at night?
* How many naps is she taking each day?
* What is the total amount of sleep she is getting via daily naps?
* What is the total amount of sleep my child is getting each day/night?
* What is the recommended amount of sleep for my child based on her age? (It is usually somewhere between ten and twelve hours.)
* Have I really tried everything? Have you experimented with making changes to elements of the routine, such as giving her a night-light, making the bedroom darker, warmer, colder, noisier, or quieter? Take into account that satisfying dinners, plenty of exercise during the day, and more or less parental closeness at night could make for a better night's sleep.
* Am I giving my child enough time to transition from playtime to bed or nap times? Similarly, has she been awake long enough from her last nap to be ready for bedtime? Bedtime won't go well if your child is wound up or genuinely not tired due to having napped too late. See the bedtime routine section on page 52 for more on this.
* Does my child seem tired? Is she happy?
* Why am I unhappy with my child's current sleep schedule? Questions to contemplate might be: Is she sleeping enough but not at the hours I would like her to be sleeping through? Does she go to bed and wake up at the perfect time but wake many times during the night? Is she going to bed too late and waking up early?

In answering these questions, you should begin to feel a greater sense of control as problem areas reveal themselves. Most likely, you will have noted something you would like to change about the timing of your child's sleep as well as one or two situational, be it behavioral or environmental, aspects of your child's sleep routine that you feel need to change.

Creating a routine

The second step requires answering two questions: What type of sleep schedule would be best for my child? What aspects of her routine should I begin to experiment with? For more guidance, however, refer to the next section, creating a sleep schedule, on page 48. In this step you will commit to certain times for bedtime routine, bedtime, wake-up, and nap/s. I would recommend allotting time for a bedtime routine because it will take most children, on average, about an hour to unwind. If you don't plan for it, you may find your lights-off time happens later than you'd hoped. How you spend this bedtime-routine hour is up to you. Commonly, it's a time for bathing, teeth brushing, and books.

If you are using a sleep schedule and bedtime routine that are reasonable (i.e. that take into account the child's sleep needs, rather than trying to force them onto a schedule that might be preferable to the parents,) then you're on the right track and this might be enough. I was certainly content just to have more control over Keli's sleep schedule. If you've gotten some control over this but are still having problems, you may be dealing with night waking. Look back to question five in your sleep assessment. Environmental changes may be the cause and these are quite easy to fix with a bit of experimenting. If your little one is still waking at night, tips from the poor-sleep culprits section on page 54 may be helpful.

Creating a Sleep Schedule

After asking your child's age, a new-parent friend's next question is likely to be, "What's his schedule?" This is a common topic of conversation if your children are the same age, and very often specifically refers to wake-up, nap, and bedtimes. New parents are interested in the big "S" because no matter how much you try to come up with the perfect sleep schedule, there is always a flaw. In the world of babies and sleep, one mistake can determine how the entire day will go, so we are desperate to figure it out.

A key concern is that our children are staying up later than we want them to; we're not sure why they won't go to bed at seven-thirty on the dot like all the other kids. Yet, while we're busy focusing on bedtime, naptime sneaks in to ruin the show. I found that the most surprising aspect of trying to get my daughter on a decent sleep schedule was the extreme significance of her naptime. Everything revolved around this. If your child is going to bed too late, it's because he's napping too late. As a result, he sleeps in later and then naps too late again the next day. The good news is that this cycle is easily broken.

If your child is napping twice a day

You will need to observe what I call his "up times." Figure out how long he stays awake between waking and his first nap, and between his first and second nap. You might want to document these times in a journal for a few days to see if there's a pattern. Next, prepare yourself for some math.

Once you have this information, you have the power to set a bedtime, waking, and naptime schedule that starts at the time you'd like your child to go to sleep. A baby or toddler usually needs approximately eleven hours. Pick the bedtime you'd like for your child and set the wake-up time eleven hours later (see examples on page 50.)

From there, choose two naptimes that will work for your child. If your son sleeps for eleven hours at night, you are aiming to fit two naps into thirteen hours. Given your child's up times, is this possible? Do the math and if there aren't enough hours in the day for two naps, consider dropping a nap from the schedule. If there is enough time, yet your child's schedule isn't working, inconsistency is the likely culprit. You need to focus on being strict about the bedtime hour and make sure he is going down at the times you chose for his naps. This requires a lot of preparation and attention on your part, but it's just a phase. Soon he'll be down to one simple nap.

Transitioning from two to one naps

You might begin to suspect that it's time to drop a nap if your child is between ten and thirteen months and stays up increasingly late at night. If you're aiming for the ideal bedtime of between 7 p.m. and 8 p.m., your older baby needs to be awake from his nap by 2 p.m. Dropping a nap doesn't mean you literally abandon the second nap and then carry on with the first nap or vice versa, but that you merge both naps at a mid-point during the day.

A child that has been getting two naps is likely going down for that first nap quite early and will need to adjust to a later first nap; otherwise he won't make it through dinner. You'll find that when he does finally sleep, he'll be more tired than usual and will sleep for a longer stretch. Ideally, this nap will be between 11 a.m. and 2 p.m. The trick is in keeping him happy until his new naptime. I found that taking Keli outside or to a new place was good for this. Going for a swim is a great idea: there's nothing like pool fun to keep your little one wide-awake. In the beginning, there will be some days when he isn't able to keep up with your new plan.

That's okay: there will be setbacks because sleep works in cycles, but you can try it again the next day. Try not to be discouraged—before you know it, he will have adjusted perfectly to this new schedule.

If your little one is down to one nap a day and is going to bed too late

It's easier to adjust your child's schedule if he's down to one nap than when he is still taking two or three naps. If you're reading this, I wouldn't be surprised if your child has been going to bed as late as 11 p.m. for weeks. First it was 9 p.m., then 10 p.m., and suddenly you have a little night owl on your hands. He likely wakes as late as 9 a.m. the next morning and has the first nap far too late at around 2 p.m. Children tend to have a longer waking period after their nap than they do after their morning wake-up. An older baby taking a nap at 2 p.m. will stay up too late.

How to break this cycle? Wake your little one up at 7 a.m. He will nap earlier and therefore be ready for bed earlier. Nobody wants to wake a child up in the morning before he's ready, but this is the only way to reset his internal clock. Prepare for this early wake-up: arrange nice activities, have an exciting morning treat readily available, and be aware that you may have a grouchy few hours until that first nap, which is perfectly normal.

Two-naps-a-day example schedule:

✳ 7.30 a.m. wake.

✳ 10.30 a.m.–11.30 a.m. nap.

✳ 3 p.m.–4.30 p.m. nap.

✳ 8.30 p.m. bedtime.

One-nap-a-day example schedule:

✳ 7 a.m. wake.

✳ 11 a.m.–2 p.m. nap.

✳ 8 p.m. bedtime.

If your little one is down to one nap a day but is waking up too early

Your little one is ready for bed at 5 p.m. and wakes at 3 a.m. to play. You're doing all you can to keep his head out of the mashed potatoes you made for dinner and you've been dealing with meltdowns for the past hour. What does it mean? If your little one is waking before 6 a.m., he's ready to nap and be awake again as early as 10 or 11 a.m. If he's been awake for six or seven hours by dinnertime, naturally he will be exhausted. The solution is challenging but it generally works really well.

On a day that you're feeling brave, plan fun activities, let your child have a chocolate chip cookie, and do all you can to keep your exhausted child from napping until at least 11 a.m. (later you'll move this to noon.) He will be so tired by then that he'll sleep later, maybe until 2 p.m. Waking up later should be enough to keep him alert until a more reasonable bedtime hour.

A Good Bedtime Routine

Does your child really need a bedtime routine? Why can't you just wait until she is exhausted and put her down expecting that she'll drift off twenty minutes later? Maybe you know better than I did, but these were the types of questions I asked when I first heard about bedtime routines. I thought they were something certain parents did to be even more routine-oriented, the type of parents who feed, change, and bathe their babies on a tight schedule, and that it was all about control. I was very wrong.

I didn't know that by never allowing my child an hour to unwind, I was allowing her to become overtired and unable to drift off when her actual bedtime came. A bedtime routine is a way to get your child to go to her bedroom without fighting you; after all, it's just story time. More importantly, it's an hour of relaxation so that she is physically more capable of sleep when the lights are turned off. By removing the struggle and helping your child to relax before bedtime, she could gain one to two more hours of sleep per night.

✳ HELPFUL HINTS

1 The routine needs to be consistent. Whatever you plan to do for the hour before bed, do it every single night. If you budge, you will find your child playing jump rope. If you budge, you will find her challenging you about whether or not she really does have to brush her teeth after her bath.

2 The routine should be pleasant. If your routine consists of bathing, teeth brushing, pajama dressing, and one book, then your child may feel as if her bedtime routine is more about bedtime than relaxing. Try to mix it up a bit. Try increasing the number of books or creating a nest for her to lie in for storytelling. She may want to invite stuffed-animal friends to reading time or spend the last ten minutes before lights off playing a word game with you. We play I spy sometimes. As long as it's quiet and calm it should be okay.

3 The routine needs to be at least one hour long and made up of two parts. The first part is made up of the necessary before-bed preparations, mainly hygiene, and should be kept to thirty minutes at most. The second part is the relaxing and connecting time. You might choose reading, singing, massage, or storytelling for the relaxing part of the routine.

4 Your bedtime routine should take place in a relaxing environment. It should be dim, quiet, peaceful, and free of toys.

5 Start it at the same reasonable time every night. You can't expect your little one to sleep by eight in the evening if her last nap lasted until four in the afternoon. Whatever time you choose, put her actual sleep needs above your need for her to sleep.

Why Won't my Baby Sleep?

You may start to lose hope if you've implemented a good bedtime routine and a set schedule based on sleep requirements and are still having a hard time getting your baby or toddler to sleep. While for most parents this is usually enough, if some of the basic changes offered in the last section haven't worked, you may need to look at the more complex sleep issues a child can have. In this section I deal with some of the other causes of poor sleep and offer solutions to them. This is not a comprehensive list, but these culprits are among the most common.

Not having a bedtime routine

A bedtime routine helps your child unwind, sets his internal clock, and tells him what to expect so as to avoid battles. Suggestions for implementing a bedtime routine are given in the previous section.

Ensuring that your child gets plenty of fresh air and exercise during the day will expend energy and help your child to sleep at night.

Inconsistent sleep schedule

This is when you allow your child to sleep in when he is tired or stay up late for naptime when he seems rowdier than normal. I personally don't mind bending this one a little (an hour here or there can usually be worked out at the end of the night in the bedtime routine,) but if you let your child nap three hours later than usual, it will be very difficult to establish the good bedtime routine that you need. Try and get your child up at the same time every day and keep his naptimes consistent (see pages 48–51 for tips on how to do this.)

Your child is overtired

This occurs either because you give in to your child's desire to stay up late or you are strict about bedtime but he stays up late battling you over it. The solution is a bedtime routine that ends in lights out at a reasonable time (between 7 and 8.30 p.m., remembering the last nap cannot go past 2.30 p.m.)

Too much television, sugar, and other stimulation

Stimulating foods, electronics, and activities such as horseplay with daddy when he comes home from work can all affect a child's ability to go to sleep at a reasonable hour. The solution is not to allow any of these activities to take

place in the last hour before bedtime. I stop Keli's sugar intake after her last nap of the day. It will also be difficult for your child to prepare for sleep if the room is too stimulating. Make sure that your child's bedroom is dimly lit, quiet, and toy-free.

Not enough daily exercise

If your child was lethargic, bored, and under-stimulated all day, he might begin playing at bedtime. Try to give your child two hours of outdoor play everyday. When that's not possible, a dance party, pillow mountain, or turning your mattress into a slide are good indoor ways for him to expend energy.

Your child won't go to bed— and that's all there is to it

I strongly recommend a bedtime routine as the solution but there are ways of making this period and bedtime itself more pleasant for your child. Visit the library weekly so there's always a new book to read. Take him to the store and let him chose his own special bedtime friends, pillow, and blanket. Put these things in a "nest" (pillow and blankets zone) close to his bed. You can then say, "Let's read that new dinosaur book in your nest with tiger," rather than, "Let's go to bed." This worked for us 75 percent of the time; the other 25 percent required exhausting creativity or the classic bedtime battle.

✳ HELPFUL HINTS

Waking during the night has several causes. The most common are high need or clingy temperament, sleep associations, hunger, new milestones, discomfort, food allergies, teething, and general illness.

1 Clinginess. When we went through big life changes, bouts of separation anxiety hit Keli hard and affected the quality of her sleep. Try to keep big changes in your life to a minimum. Some kids need to know that you're there in order for them to sleep well. For this, I recommend connecting with your child during the day and co-sleeping to build security.

2 Sleep associations. The big one is nursing and it's difficult to break. Please see the breast-feeding chapter for guidance (page 60.) Some children will associate sleep with a certain type of lighting or background noise. When this is the case, try to maintain this setting throughout the night.

3 Hunger. A baby who is mostly relying on milk for calories may become hungry in the night. If your child is old enough, give him something that is filling and comforting before bed such as bananas, rice cereal, or mashed potatoes.

4 New milestones. This is a real phenomenon. A child who is working on crawling, walking, or using the potty will be more restless because this excitement—whether biological or mental—will keep him practicing at night.
Help him to work on his new milestone as much as possible during the day (the exercise tip on the previous page will also be helpful.)

5 Discomfort. Ensure that your child is appropriately dressed. If he tends to kick his covers off in the night, put warmer pajamas on him before you tuck him in for the night. If he wakes up sweating, switch to shorts, and make sure his clothing isn't too long or loose as these can get twisted up. Sensitive children in particular will wake up if they are uncomfortable.

6 Food allergies, teething, and general illnesses. Just being aware of these issues should help your state of mind a little. The decision to give your child medication or painkillers to help them sleep if they are suffering from an illness or allergy is, of course, a personal one. If you need to do this, be sure to speak to a pediatrician about appropriate medicines and doses.

Recognizing Tired and Overtired Signs

Babies don't always know when they are tired and even when they do, it doesn't necessarily follow that they will be able to self-soothe or relax enough to go to sleep. Many babies, especially Attachment-Parented babies, depend on their parents for help in falling asleep. When they become toddlers and start to be aware of feeling sleepy and are learning self-soothing skills, they begin to fight sleep because it interferes with playing and learning.

In either situation, it becomes necessary for the parents to intervene, first by being able to see when their child is ready for sleep and then by helping them to fall asleep. It is incredibly difficult to recognize the signs of both tiredness and overtiredness, and then to help a child fall asleep having recognized these signs. However, this will be necessary to ensure that your child does not become overtired.

Tired signs

* Whining
* Fussing
* Crying
* Screaming
* Excess nursing or feeding
* Yawning
* Glazed stare
* Avoiding eye contact
* Less active
* Back arching
* Pulling on face
* Facial grimaces
* Flailing legs and arms
* Rubbing eyes
* Pulling on hair or ears
* Clumsiness
* Walking backwards

Overtired signs

* Clinginess
* Screaming
* Refusing to eat
* Needs motion—walking, bouncing, rocking
* Inconsolable—hard to settle
* Frustrated—hitting, throwing things, kicking
* Naughty—oppositional, loud, biting, ignoring parents
* Hypersensitive—melts down over little things
* Hyperactive—jumping, running, climbing

I used to believe that the theory that children become overtired and therefore unable to sleep was a myth. After ignoring the advice I heard, such as "put her down even if she doesn't seem tired" or "put her down even if she's fighting it, all babies need twelve hours of sleep at night," the time came when I realized I had to do some experimenting with this theory before I dismissed it. My daughter's sleep was erratic and she seemed tired hours before she was willing to sleep. Although I was committed to being one step ahead of my child's need for sleep, I wasn't sure how I would know for sure that she needed to sleep. I was hesitant about taking too much control because it seemed harsh to insist on her sleeping before she was ready.

A baby-led schedule

Therein lay a misunderstanding. I had the idea that schedule setting always meant the parent led rather than the child. I wanted to be baby-led and had a natural distaste for controlling her sleep and eating habits too much. But creating a sleep schedule in order to prevent overtiredness is still in line with being baby-led. It just means being more in tune with your baby's needs and not

You can create a sleep schedule without compromising on a baby-led parenting style.

waiting for her to come to the same conclusion as you. It is possible to have a sleep-friendly schedule and be an Attachment Parent. I do not recommend shutting your tired baby in her room by herself and expect her to self-soothe all for the sake of not becoming overtired. Mom and dad can be just as involved in the sleep process as ever—you just need to be ahead of the game.

An early bedtime

I discovered that an early bedtime was indeed what Keli needed. She fought this bedtime every night only to fall asleep and then sleep better than if I left her to her old habit of passing out exhausted at ten at night. I also learned that if I put her down for a nap before she was grouchy and showing other signs of overtiredness, she would nod off more easily. It turned out that the overtired theory was not a myth. What's interesting to note is that even when I put her down earlier, she did not wake up earlier: it was clear that she needed those extra hours of sleep.

Many of the signs of tiredness and overtiredness are not easy to detect and can often be mistaken for something else. By the time you notice that something is off about your child, she may already be overtired. The previous page shows the most common signs that your baby or toddler is tired or overtired (bear in mind that some of these require certain developmental gains, so look for the ones that your child is capable of as appropriate indicators.)

I wish I could conclude this section by telling you exactly what to do with your overtired baby. Your overtired baby will never be easy to get to sleep and

if she is high need or highly sensitive, the intensity of the above signs could double. I found that repetitive vertical bouncing coupled with a noise machine and making shh-ing sounds worked best for us. You will find the best solution for soothing your overtired child and, after implementing some of the advice in this sleep chapter, good habits will develop. Without knowing exactly when or how it happened, you'll see that your sleep routine has fallen into place and your home has become a happier and more smoothly run environment.

CHAPTER 3:
Breast-Feeding and Night-Weaning

Getting Started with Breast-Feeding

Much like co-sleeping, breast-feeding seemed like a best-fit practice for our family. I'm going to assume that my readers are already fully convinced that breast-feeding is a wonderful way to provide nutrients for your child. As wonderful as it is, however (you probably know what's coming,) it's not always particularly easy to adopt or as natural as it seems from a distance.

Some mothers will make the decision to breast-feed, but bottle-feeding may be, or become, necessary due to unpredictable physical complications. Breast-feeding only begins with a decision and then nature will decide the ultimate course of our experience. It's important to manage your expectations—should you not be able to breast-feed, don't compare yourself to others, and keep in mind that you are still an Attachment Parent.

We're a low-fuss family; we like to fuss over the important things and not let life's little things interrupt the flow of an otherwise balanced day. Buying bottles, sterilizing them, spending thousands of dollars on formula, preparing bottles while my baby is hungry, packing enough milk for outings, and standing, half conscious, over the kitchen counter at two in the morning mixing formula all seemed like a lot of extra work to me. However, although I am very grateful for our success with breast-feeding Keli, it wasn't as convenient as I'd imagined it would be, at least not in the beginning.

A plethora of information about breast-feeding has been published, so I will avoid going into extensive how-to instructions. The best thing you can do as you get started with breast-feeding is to read as much as you can. Of the books currently available I recommend *The Food of Love* by Kate Evans; this will give you all of the how-to-information that you need. Cultivate a mood of awareness, education, and surrender and you will be off to a great start.

✳ HELPFUL HINTS

1 A good "latch" is when your baby's bottom lip is under the areola and his chin is pressed into the bottom half of your breast. A newborn may need some support from you in order to press his head into that grip so that he can get the right latch. This will help keep him from sucking on only the nipple. There will be some variation depending on the size of your breast, nipple, and your baby's mouth.

2 It's useful to learn how your breasts make milk, especially what slows down and increases milk production. Find out what you can take if your supply has dropped, or be ahead of the game and avoid anything that can reduce your milk supply. Be aware that an oversupply of milk can be burdensome too—familiarize yourself with the symptoms and what to do should you have either low or overabundant milk supplies.

3 Be aware of possible breastfeeding complications. Should anything make breast-feeding more difficult for you, you'll want to be able to recognize the problem and begin to troubleshoot it immediately. I recommend keeping a nipple cream that is made of lanolin in your medicine cabinet for the entirety of your breast-feeding days. At the first sign of soreness, apply and leave covered for a couple of hours. Lanolin will soothe sore nipples before your next nursing. (However, please note that lanolin is not suitable if you are sensitive to wool.)

4 The emotional and physical demands of nursing are trying, and both baby and mother require an adjustment period. Your baby will oftentimes fall asleep in your arms (maybe more often than not.) Have a one-armed plan for eating, such as a supply of finger foods. You may want to have a tablet computer as they are easy to use and you'll want some entertainment for these long stretches. I also urge new mothers to begin considering the emotional impact of nursing a child (especially when you nurse on demand.) Ask yourself if you're ready to wake up all through the night, be glued to your couch for hours on end, to wean a toddler, or nurse in public.

5 Nip bad nursing habits in the bud immediately. Keli likes to twist on the nipple that she is not drinking from. Aside from hurting a little bit, this seemed harmless at first and it obviously helped to calm her down. Now, she is not a happy, comfortable little nurser unless she has full access to both breasts at one time. There are a lot of situations where this is very difficult and in almost all situations, it's not comfortable for me. The first time your child does this be sure to pull their hand away. Other bad habits include kicking while nursing, being wild, pulling your shirt up on a whim, or pulling on hair.

Breast-Feeding Myths

A long list of parenting challenges awaits new parents, many of which they will prepare for and when they arise, face them head on. We all anticipate sleepless, teething nights, dread the first shampoo in the eyes, and know that weaning will be difficult. However, breast-feeding doesn't always make the list and it can sometimes be an unwelcome surprise to realize that it is far from easy. This section looks at some of the most prevalent myths and misconceptions surrounding breast-feeding.

2 **There's no way to know if the breast is empty.** I'm still stumped by the fact that I consulted at least three lactation experts, thirty websites, and fifteen friends before learning how to know when my baby needed to be switched to the other breast. Look at your child's jaw while she nurses. You will see it moves quickly up and down a few times (as if she was chewing bubblegum,) then it will drop lower and come back up more slowly: that is precisely when milk is being swallowed. If you only see the "chewing bubblegum" jaw it means you should switch breasts.

1 **Having an overabundant milk supply is a good problem to have.** Although an overabundant milk supply is a better problem to have than a low supply, oversupply can lead to difficulties and deserves some attention, too. One cause of colic can be an oversupply of milk. If your child is drinking too much foremilk (a problem specific to an oversupply of milk,) is gagging on milk (hence sucking in excess air,) or is getting too full from overeating, then colic-like symptoms can develop and persist. Getting too much foremilk can also cause diarrhea. Your child may become fussy while eating or disinterested in nursing because it is an unpleasant experience. Block feeding can be helpful to remedy this situation.

3 **Your breast might leak a little; here's a nipple pad.** I kept thinking this would cease and I just wasn't prepared for it. The name "nipple pad" is misleading: forget nipple pads, you're going to need nipple towels! Your T-shirt, your bed, and your baby might be covered in milk for many nights. The last thing a new sleep-deprived mom needs is to get up and put on a dry shirt, but if you're like me, you'll need to do it often. Come up with a solution as soon as you discover that this may be a nuisance. I was too stubborn to find a good solution thinking that any day now it would just end.

4   Your breasts will never be empty.

One-minute expert-lactation sources tell you it is time to switch your baby to the other breast and then in the same breath tell you that your breasts are never truly empty. It is utterly confusing and stressful to know both of these "facts." If there's not enough milk to satisfy my daughter, I consider my breasts to be empty. Yes, there may be some milk somewhere in the factory but if she can't get what she needs or wants, then I need to know about it. It would help me to understand why she's cranky: maybe she's hungry, perhaps she's not getting the milk she's used to getting to help her sleep, maybe she's frustrated that my breasts are empty, or the opposite—perhaps there is plenty of milk, so hunger can't be the problem. This myth rules out all of these very real possibilities and makes a woman think that her child could never be hungry.

Any woman who has tried to express milk has had the experience of not being able to get the milk out. Hormones affect milk supply, as can teething, which may result in non-stop nursing that effectively "empties" the breasts. The same is true for hunger caused by growth spurts. The persistence of this myth means that there isn't much advice available to help you understand how to recognize and handle this situation (see myth 2 for a possible solution.)

5   Breast-feeding babies get all of the nutrients they need from breast milk.

We are always told that the mother's milk will provide the baby with everything she needs. That's almost true, except for iron. Formula-fed babies get plenty of iron because formulas are fortified with iron. Breast milk often does not supply a child with the necessary amount of iron after she has reached about six months. At this age, her iron stores begin to get used up and the daily requirement for iron increases beyond what a mother's milk can supply.

6 **Once you've nursed your child to sleep, you can put her down.** Needless to say, you'd rather not have your sleeping child on you, especially if you are sleepy too, but many babies will wake up when put down. I was stuck with a sleeping baby on my lap countless times, so eventually I lay down in my bed while nursing. That way, I wouldn't have to put her down at all. In order to get her unlatched (because some babies just won't let go,) I used the "Pantley Pull-Off" method, as described in *The No-Cry Sleep Solution*. I discovered another trick that was helpful when Keli was hard to move away from me. If your child is nursing and not willing to give up the breast, it's quite possible that she's just feeling tense and needs help to relax. Find where she holds tension: shoulders, between the eyes, legs, etc. In a gentle, circular motion massage the tension out with your thumb or hand. You will feel your child relaxing and the grip on your nipple will become lighter. If you do this as she is falling asleep you may be surprised to find that she even drops the nipple.

7 **Your child will self-wean.** If you're on the fence about whether or not to wean your child, you've likely consulted the Internet for advice. Passionate breast-feeding advocates will gently remind us that no matter how tiring it is there is an end in sight. I am one of those but would like to remind you that the end may not be in sight. That your child will eventually self-wean is of course true, but it is also misleading: a child might not self-wean until she is five years old. If you're not comfortable with waiting that long, you might want to consider letting go of the self-wean promise. It is common to hear that a child who is allowed to continue breast-feeding on demand will do so well into her third or fourth year. If I had known that Keli could be waking up five to ten times a night to nurse for the first two years of her life, I might have night-weaned her sooner. This, potentially, would have been easier on both of us than waiting for her to self-wean.

Preparing to Night-Wean

If you flipped to these pages, you are most likely tired and frustrated: First, let me say, I am sorry. The only person who can be truly sorry while being a complete stranger to you is another sleep-deprived mother or one who has been there. You are so incredibly, painfully tired and yet you will not sleep tonight. You know this already even though it's only eight o'clock in the morning. You know you will be awoken one to ten times tonight and the thought of it is torturous. Maybe it's time to night-wean.

Night-weaning is the process of introducing new methods to the nighttime routine that will eventually lead to your child no longer nursing when he wakes up in the middle of the night. This increases the likelihood that he will stop waking altogether or that if he does wake, he will soothe himself back to sleep. The end result is that you both get a full night's sleep.

Deciding to night-wean

There are many ways to introduce and follow through with weaning. It seems that most people find it easier to day-wean and then go to night-weaning. These are parents who are interested in fully weaning their child. A lot of women are completely content to nurse into toddlerhood while waiting for their child to self-wean, but find that all-through-the-night feeding must come to a halt because they feel they will fall to pieces if they don't get a decent night's sleep soon.

Initially, I believed that Keli would eventually self-wean and I was keen to let her lead the way. However, this led to both of us being sleep deprived. We woke between four and eight times a night (sometimes more) for full-on nursing sessions.

If my milk supply was low on a particular night, Keli would become frustrated and nurse hysterically for two hours at a time. Nursing at night began to feel more like a nightmare than a positive connection.

Given the freedom to choose, Keli would still be nursing at night as she nears her third birthday. Some will suggest that night weaning is not an Attachment Parenting practice, but I believe that anything (when done with gentle consideration for your child's needs and emotional state) can be Attachment-Parenting friendly. If you feel it would be detrimental to your child's needs to stop nursing, then please don't stop. But if he is secure, old enough to connect with you in different ways, and can understand the reason behind your new boundaries, then it's okay to wean.

Keeping the AP bond

Being AP mothers, we sacrifice free time, date nights with our husbands, one third of our beds, and the upper half of our bodies for our baby's happiness. This is all part of Attachment Parenting. Most of us will also sacrifice sleep and that's okay, to a point. Suffering from fatigue, depression, moodiness, and low energy should not be a part of your Attachment-Parent practice. In the following sections, I will teach you how to night-wean in a way that adheres to Attachment-Parenting principles. I can say with complete confidence that mine and Keli's bond was not affected during our night-weaning process.

✳ HELPFUL HINTS

1 **Follow basic guidelines for promoting good sleep for your baby.** If you are planning to night-wean, then your child is not sleeping through the night. Perhaps he's waking up to nurse, but there could be another cause and nursing is simply how he goes back to sleep. I recommend reading the chapter on sleep (pages 36–59) because night-weaning will be unsuccessful if other factors are contributing to your child's night waking.

2 **Nurse more during the day.** This accomplishes two things: First, it fills up your child's belly in case hunger is the reason he's waking. Secondly, it helps your child to feel more secure. The more you connect with him before the sun sets, the less he will need to wake up throughout the night seeking reassurance that you are right there.

3 **Be sensitive and responsive during nursing marathons.** There will be times when your child seems to nurse constantly. Sometimes this will be due to boredom or habit, but other times he may be going through something emotional or physical and require extra nursing as a way of coping. It's important to be sensitive to higher-need times such as life changes, separation anxiety, teething, and illness. When you are responsive, your child will feel less anxious about nursing and probably sleep better at night.

4 **If you are nursing and you drink coffee in the day, I'd advise you stop.** While there is no specific research to prove this, it seems likely that there is a correlation between a nursing mother who drinks more than one cup of coffee daily and a baby with poor sleeping habits.

5 **Start talking to your child about night-weaning.** You can do this simply by saying, "One day, when you're a big boy, you won't need to nurse anymore," or "In a few more days, we're going to stop nursing at night." You can be as creative or straightforward as you want in letting your child know about night-weaning. We read *Nursies when the Sun Shines* by Katherine Havener and it was a fantastic help in preparing Keli for night-weaning.

6 **Talk to your partner about night-weaning.** Children are not the only ones who become accustomed to the nighttime routine. Making these changes will be challenging and result in a temporary loss of sleep for everyone. Make sure that you and your partner agree that the timing is right and that you are supported in choosing and sticking to the chosen strategies.

7 **If you're co-sleeping with your child, give him more space.** Keli woke less when we were not bumping into each other all night. Giving her more space meant that the "milkies" also became less convenient. Thus began a slightly

new routine to night waking where she had to put more effort into nursing by having to find me first and then crawl over to me.

8 Break the breast-sleep association.

You might be thinking, "If I knew how to break the breast-sleep association, we wouldn't need to night-wean," but that's only partially true. Getting your child to be able to fall asleep without the breast is a little different than teaching him to accept sleeping without nursing. For now, you just need to be sure that he has other ways to help him fall asleep. And even if he still uses nursing as a way to fall asleep, once he is asleep use the "Pantley-Pull-Off" method (see page 66) to remove the nipple. This will help him get used to sleeping while not latched and most likely he'll do some tossing and turning in the night without latching back on. This is a (baby) step in the right direction.

9 Try new sleep aid techniques in the middle of the night occasionally.

Instead of teaching your child new ways to fall asleep at the beginning of the night (which tends to go poorly and not feel gentle,) move this practice to the middle of the night. I always nurse Keli to sleep at the beginning of the night, but I taught her different ways to fall asleep when she woke in the middle of the night and was already half asleep. Most often I would

pat her on the bottom, resulting in gentle vertical rocking until she fell asleep. (See the self-soothing section on page 76 for more techniques.)

10 Introduce the language you will be using for "no milk."

You can practice this at different times of the day. Maybe it's midday and your child wants to nurse. Let him, but then after ten minutes say the following: "Milkies need a break to make more milk, let's play with your felt board." Or if you're doing this while practicing new night-waking techniques say, "Oh, milkies are not helping us to rest right now, I have a new idea..." Others to try are: "Milk needs to sleep" and "No milk until the sun comes up." Say these things sweetly and optimistically and avoid any new changes while you're feeling frustrated.

A word of encouragement. Sometimes, the new techniques worked better than nursing to help Keli sleep. In doing all of the above, I became confident that she could get to sleep in many different ways. As time passed, she learned that some of these techniques were better for her at different times. Nursing can be a magical go-to-sleep tool but it can also be playful, distracting, or frustrating for babies.

Night-Weaning in Seven Days

Without clear intention, our night-weaning process was a hybrid of those that focus primarily on pacing and those that concentrate on gentle strategies for eliminating night feeds. I didn't come across anything that completely resonated with me. Although I read great books that contained night-weaning tips, they didn't suggest any real processes for implementing them; there was no time frame, the tips weren't gentle enough, and they were missing the no-cry element that I needed.

I began to believe that what was needed was a night-weaning plan that included the following: a time frame so that one could better conceptualize the process, extra gentle strategies, and room for individualization. "How I Night Weaned in Seven Days" was created in the hopes of providing readers with a well-rounded night-weaning plan. I'm not suggesting that you also night-wean in seven days. The following pacing worked for us and on the last day, my daughter slept through the night without waking. Had she not, I would have slowed down, spending as many nights as needed until she had adjusted.

Make sure to practice the tips from the previous section before getting started. Being prepared for night-weaning is in itself a challenge and having that practice will give you more confidence and will pave the way to your success here.

Days 1–3
The deal

When your child wakes up in the middle of the night, do not nurse her. What? How can this be the right thing to do in the first few days? You already know that your child can sleep off the breast, the language is in place, you've told her the plan, so what else is there to do but start night-weaning? Don't worry, I came up with something to make this much easier. I call it "the deal." It works best with toddlers but can work with babies, too. The deal gives your child an opportunity to sleep before nursing, but you won't force it. When she wakes up, simply say to her, "Right now the milkies are making milk, you have to wait a few minutes and then I'll nurse you." Keli understood this and fought a little the first night, but quickly fell into the routine of waiting before she nursed. This is the exact opposite of the popular "nurse and then soothe" trick. This is soothe and then nurse (for soothing tricks see pages 76–79.)

By the second night, the magic began. She knew she would be nursed after waiting a few minutes, so she wasn't anxious (even if still fussy.) Because of this, she began to fall asleep in the middle of the deal, before she got to nurse. If at any time your child starts reacting to the deal more intensely, take this as a sign to shorten the waiting time. If she becomes anxious, you may want to use this trick only for half of the wake-ups and for the other half nurse as usual. Keeping these first three days as peaceful as possible is the goal.

By the third night, Keli was perfectly fine with this situation, most of the time falling asleep before the waiting time was up. Other times she stayed awake until I was willing to nurse her. I know she was feeling secure throughout all of this because after she nursed, she would roll away from me to get more comfortable and then fall asleep. She didn't seem tense or anxious and, most

importantly, her behavior and disposition were all fine the next day. Part of night-weaning is making nursing inconvenient. The deal works wonderfully for that.

In the case of babies, you obviously can't tell them about the deal, but you could just make them wait five minutes before nursing them.

Days 4–6
No milkies

Now you start to say "no milkies" in the way that you've decided to explain it to your child after reading the previous section. Be consistent—say the same thing each time and explain it in the simplest terms because small children can't understand much more than the "no" part. If your little one is resistant, your normal soothing tricks may not be enough. On the first night, I had to pick up Keli, walk her around the room a bit, cradle her, and explain to her very gently that she would get milk when the sun came up. She was upset, but she felt safe and loved in my arms. If you don't have to pick up your child, don't. It's important to stay calm and keep the sleep environment as normal as possible.

I noticed that because I had taken the milk away entirely, her previous attitude to trying to get herself back to sleep had changed. Once there was no milk, she was less cooperative and more demanding. She wanted to be cradled and carried for the first time since she was a baby. Day four was the hardest. Keli cried and fussed pretty intensely for ten minutes. Yes, it was only ten minutes,

but at night that felt like a long time. This was then followed by an hour of her asking me to soothe her in other ways, once or twice trying to get the milkies again, and a few more tears. Prepare yourself for it and really concentrate on being calm and optimistic. Everyone will make it through this night just fine. Eventually, she fell asleep.

Keli woke a few more times on night four and asked to nurse, but there were no tears and she didn't fuss much for the rest of that night. On nights five and six she didn't ask for milk at all. On night five she had some trouble sleeping and would ask me to hold her or hold her hand. She knew that she had to go to sleep without nursing and also that I was there to help her. It's important to agree to anything your child needs. By night six she woke just once and didn't ask to nurse. To my surprise, even when she was trying her hardest and no longer asking for milk, she struggled to self-settle. This was no longer a resistance issue, but she actually lacked the skills that I thought she had.

I told her I would give her a present in the morning for being brave and working so hard. Each morning she would wake up and ask, "Do I get a present for not doing the milkies?" She woke up chipper and unaffected by her nighttime endeavor and I started to feel proud about something I had gone into with quite a bit of trepidation.

Day 7
Self-soothing

On day seven Keli slept through the entire night. If all goes well, your child won't be waking anymore. It's common for some children to continue to wake up for a while longer. If your child is not asking for milk anymore or she accepts "no" without any tears or a fight, then your night weaning is going really well. The only difference with night seven and those that follow is that you should shorten the length of time you spend helping your little one get back to sleep. Do the soothing techniques for up to fifteen minutes, then stop and give her some space and see what happens. If the teaching of the self-soothing element is left out, then you've only done half your job in helping her to sleep through the night. Day seven might turn into days eight and nine, but the important thing is that your child is not drinking milk at night and is well on her way to self-soothing.

General guidelines

All throughout our process I talked to my daughter during the day about my expectations for the night and kept a close, loving connection. At night I slept close to her.

It's important to go into this process knowing that there are three good reasons to stop if you need to, and to set limits before you get started:

* If it affects your child's daytime personality and well-being.

* If after a week of doing this, she reacts as intensely with meltdowns as before and is not making any progress in this area.

* If the night waking continues for months and months, showing that your child is just a night-waker and cutting night nursings is resulting in less sleep.

Night-Weaning Reflections

When I began night weaning, I thought I knew as much as there was to know. I was armed with conviction that it was the right time to start, as well as a long list of gentle night-weaning tips. However, right in the middle of it, I realized there were all sorts of things that I needed to work on.

✳ HELPFUL HINTS

1 **Real self-soothing needs to be learned while in the process of night-weaning.** Breaking the breast-sleep association only encouraged partial self-soothing and it wasn't until I took night feeds away completely from Keli that I saw that she needed more practice with soothing than I had previously believed.

2 **Thanks to lesson number one, I realized that night-weaning can be accomplished before night waking ceases.** I had thought the two would occur simultaneously, but after Keli accepted the "no milkies" norm, we still woke to take care of her until she learned to become more independent. Fortunately, this took just a few days but it could take longer for others.

3 **It's okay to stop if it's not going well.** I avoided night-weaning for much longer than I should have because it felt so all-or-nothing to me. This isn't true, but do be careful not to quit when it gets tough. If you set limits for yourself and your child ahead of time, you can make your decisions based on those rational limits.

4 **If you're not feeling confident, try to find some success stories online.** After reading some of these, I realized that Keli can do this. She adjusted to other changes after a few days of fighting me. Having that confidence made me less anxious and upset so I handled each waking better, which improved her reaction.

5 **It's important not to take the crying and anger personally.** If you've been baby-led up until now, your child will be likely to react strongly to suddenly not getting what he wants. This reaction stems from feeling disappointed and angry. One mom told me that her child would hit her breasts when her milk supply was low. This is a perfect example to show how a child's frustration can be separate from actually blaming you.

6 **You cannot prepare too much.** I thought I had prepared Keli but I could have done a little bit more. Before actually saying "no" I needed to tell her it was going to happen. I didn't tell her on the fourth day that she was not getting "milkies" that night, nor did I have a full plan to help her self-soothe.

7 **Sleeping closer during night-weaning is a good idea.** To prepare your child for night-weaning, you'll want to create some space between you and him in the family bed. This will encourage less night waking and a bit of independence. However, while you're night-weaning, try staying close. It quickly became clear that Keli was going to do better with this while snug against me.

8 **Choose your "no milkies" language carefully.** Although "milkies are making more milk" worked really well for the deal phase of our night weaning, it didn't really carry over to the "no milkies phase." Make sure that your statement makes sense and that your child won't question or challenge it later.

Self-Soothing Tricks

Self-soothing is a main component of your child sleeping through the night. Whether you are a cry-it-out type of parent, a nursing-all-through-the-night parent, or somewhere in the middle, there will come a day when teaching your child self-soothing skills will become necessary. How much you actively do this with your child or leave up to her will depend on your parenting style.

AP parents don't sleep-train, so we don't tend to think self-soothing applies to us. But soothing tricks are just as important as gentle weaning tips. When I researched self-soothing tips, I didn't find anything that appealed to me. Where was self-soothing AP-style advice? After all, everyone needs to learn to self-soothe someday.

I'm writing specifically about teaching your child to self-soothe once she has been told that nursing to sleep is no longer an option. Teaching this skill in the middle of the night is best for two reasons: a) Your child is very sleepy already and wants to go back to sleep, and b) What more important time is there for her to be able to get back to sleep than in the middle of the night?

Keli is very aware of her own needs; once I'd removed the milk from her nighttime sleep routine, she began asking me to help comfort her back to sleep. Some of these soothing ideas came from her, some I have come up with myself, and others are as ancient as can be. The important message in this section is that if you are night-weaning, your child will need these skills. I highly recommend that you help your child soothe using the tricks below, but that you progress slowly to the tips that require your child's independence. You'll need to decide (lovingly) when your child is ready simply to be told, "Go back to sleep, honey" after a quick pat. She might surprise you and just start self-soothing after a few days of your guidance.

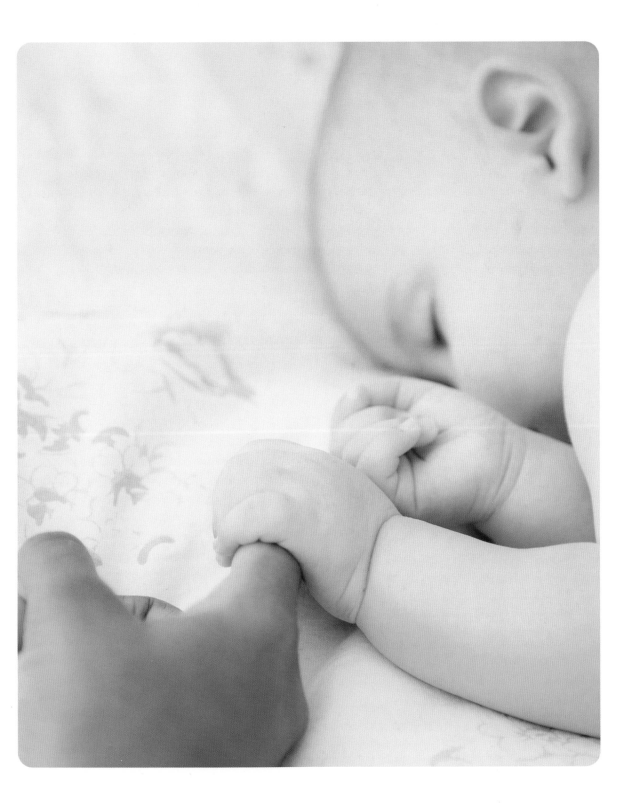

✳ HELPFUL HINTS

1 Encourage your child to close her eyes.
Keli truly didn't know how to close her eyes. She tried to; she squeezed them up so hard it was laughable. Place your hand gently and lightly over your child's eyes and sing to her. Another option is to rub your fingers gently over her eyebrows in a motion that makes the eyes want naturally to close.

2 Pat your child's back or bottom. For some reason, Keli responds best to being on her belly and having her bottom patted in a way that

also gives her a gentle vertical bounce. I've probably spent hours doing this. This rocking-up-and-down motion is recommended by Harvey Karp, author of *The Happiest Baby on the Block*, and it really works.

3 Sing. Yes, it seems old fashioned and just for babies, but my two-year-old will stay restless through all sorts of tricks until I add a simple repetitive song, then off she goes. Sometimes she request songs from me to help her to sleep. She's very aware that I am helping her sleep and appreciates the effort. At those times I'll sing something such as "Close your eyes little baby, it's time to rest, close your eyes little baby, go to sleep."

4 Cradle and rock. I sit up, put Keli on my lap, and rock her. She asks for this and will often fall asleep very quickly in my arms. Then I put her down.

5 Rub back. This is like patting but more soothing and calming, so a better option than patting when your child seems particularly tense or worked up. Rub your child's back in big circles creating warmth and rhythm. Apply a little pressure to soften her limbs and encourage relaxation.

6 Rub neck and shoulders. One day I realized that Keli holds tension in her shoulders. I did the exact same thing as before but closer to her shoulders and upper-back, and I could feel her body relax under my hand almost instantly. Try massaging different parts of your child's body until you find a spot that seems to calm her quickly.

7 Hold her hand. This seemed silly to me when my friend suggested it, but Keli did actually ask to hold my hand (several times) when I was night-weaning her.

8 Cuddle. You may think that cuddling could never replace nursing, but one day it will. Your newly night-weaned child will often want to sleep under your arm or use your neck as a pillow. This sounds terrible, but she probably won't fall asleep this way. Cuddling will help your child to relax before she goes to sleep.

9 Give your child a bottle, teether, teddy bear, or blanket. These can encourage self-soothing initially. However, I don't recommend prolonged use because they are really just sleep aids. These items shouldn't be considered security items— your little one has her mommy for that, full time. When Keli was feeling restless and unsure of what to do with her hands or arms, I realized that she would benefit from a small distraction. I gave her a teddy bear, which she enjoyed bouncing

on her belly, and a bottle of water that she enjoyed chewing on. Both of these helped her to unwind and relax.

10 Give your child some space. The tips above promote and teach self-soothing but they will not make your child a self-soother straightaway. Practice each night, gradually lessening the amount of time you spend on them. You will notice that your child needs this help less frequently and will start taking to the tricks that depend on you less. When you think she is ready, do these tricks but then say, "It's time to go night-night," and leave her to go to sleep on her own.

Will your Toddler ever Self-Wean? (Just for Fun)

Forget signs of readiness. We're counting up the signs of un-readiness here: The decision about weaning is often a hard one for mothers. If we're thinking about weaning, it's most likely due to the realization that our child is not going to simply wean herself anytime soon. In other words, she is attached to nursing. While this is completely understandable, it also weighs heavy on our hearts as we consider our own needs for health, sleep, and space. I thought I'd make light of it all by discussing some of our children's most attached behaviors so that you know you're not alone. Here are some of my favorites.

1 **Your child has cleverly named your breasts** after her favorite thing in the world: herself or "me-mees."

2 **When you take your shirt off and she sees your breasts** she screams "me-mees" (or whatever your child calls them) with such enthusiasm you'd think she'd been presented with a pile of presents.

3 **When Daddy tells her it's time to go to bed,** which around here is a threat that he is doing the bedtime routine that night, she pounces onto your breast so quickly that you don't see her move.

4 **She wrote a song that she chants** at random parts of the day: "Me-mee me-mee me-mee," and also dances to it sometimes.

5 **She sometimes pulls your shirt up** just to lie on your breasts and kisses them with no intention to nurse.

6 **The words "mama" and "me-mee"** are interchangeable to her.

7 When she's tired, she grabs your nipple and rubs it in her itchy sleepy eyes for comfort.

8 She kicks "me-mees" or stands on them occasionally and, based on the "What? These are mine!" expression on her face, you're pretty sure this is a territorial thing.

9 You hide from her while getting dressed or undressed in fear that her alter ego breast-feeding-monster will manifest at any moment for the tenth random and unnecessary nursing fit of the day.

10 You running around the house with a thirty-pound child on your hip, one breast out, with her trying desperately to latch back onto it while you turn off the stove because something is boiling over, is not an uncommon sight. This was normal when she was a baby, too, but didn't look quite as ridiculous.

11 She gets a packet of sticky jewels out of a toy vending machine. You expect her to use them to decorate her face or hands, but instead she uses them to decorate your breasts and seems quite pleased that her milk supply is now dazzling.

12 She pulls out her harmonica, runs over to you, looks at your breasts, and begins to play. You are certain anyway, but you check for good measure, yes, she is playing a song just for her mee-mees.

13 She has now gotten into the habit of hugging the me-mees, which is kind of like hugging me but also different. The main way it is different is that she says, "I'm hugging the mee-mees" even though I never asked.

14 I ask her what she wants to be for Halloween and she tells me "me-mees!" and then points to one specifically and says, "This one."

15 Me-mees are a guest at our play picnics. She "feeds" them food and juice and, of course, this wouldn't be a good idea unless the me-mees got their teeth brushed afterwards. Yes, that happened, but fortunately she used an imaginary toothbrush.

CHAPTER 4:
Food and Nutrition

Introducing Solids

The introduction of solids into your child's life should be an exciting development. You hope it's true that your son will sleep better, you anticipate either a big smile or comic expression that says "no thanks" with each new food, and you feel proud that he can eat "real" food. However, despite the joys, it can be a stressful time. Some mothers feel pushed into introducing solids, either because the recommended age is six months or because well-meaning friends and family think it will be beneficial for the child. Others will choose for themselves but feel deflated when their little one meets them with resistance.

Six months is commonly listed as the ideal age for introducing solids. By this time a growing and more active baby will begin to show hunger signs and require more calories than milk alone can provide. However, it is recommended that breast milk or formula continue to be the main source of your baby's calories and nutrients until he is one. Take heart in that your child can be healthy and also turn down many meals in that first year when his food needs are mostly being met by milk.

From one AP parent to another, my advice is to go with your intuition and follow your baby's cues. This doesn't need to be a time of conflict or power struggle. If your first few attempts to serve your child rice cereal and avocado don't end well, don't give up. It may be that he isn't sure of what to do or is still satisfied by his last milk feed. The tips that follow will help you both get off to a good start. For more information on what to feed your child, see the nutrition section on pages 86–87. If your child is continuously distressed by or disinterested in solids, don't worry—try again in a few weeks.

When to introduce solids

* No earlier than six months.
* Your child can sit up independently.
* Your child has good head control.
* Extrusion reflex has disappeared (this is when your baby pushes food forward and out of his mouth with his tongue.)
* Birth weight has doubled.
* Shows interest in what you are eating.
* Shows hunger signs: fussy even after being nursed, opens mouth on seeing solids.
* You are able to offer foods other than purées, when your child demonstrates pincer grasp, can put food in his own mouth, and mashes food with gums.

How to introduce solids

✳ Start at just once a day and move up to three times daily as interest increases.

✳ Choose a time when your baby is hungry but not yet fussing to eat (as he'll probably refuse to experiment then.) I recommend thirty minutes before his next milk feed.

✳ Give your child his very first taste off your finger. This will help him to focus on the food rather than his first experience with an eating utensil.

✳ If your child has not been using a high chair, give him the first few solid feedings with him in your lap (again, to help with focusing.)

✳ Do not let your child crawl or bounce with food in his mouth as this could result in choking.

✳ To determine if your baby is allergic or has an intolerance to a particular food, give him one new food at a time and wait for three days before offering another.

✳ If he pulls back or turns his head away from the spoon, shuts his mouth, or begins to fuss, he may not be interested in solids or may no longer be hungry. Try again later.

✳ If your breast-fed child is not taking to solids by the time he is eight or nine months old, speak to your pediatrician about supplements.

What to introduce

Start with rice or oatmeal cereals and then gradually experiment with puréed fruits and vegetables. These are perfect starter foods because they are easy to swallow and digest. Some gentle fruits low in acid are pears, apples, and bananas. Mild vegetables include avocado, peas, squash, and sweet potato; you can mix fruit or vegetables into the cereals or feed them separately (take note of what your child prefers.) Feed your child appropriate foods that are rich in iron, vitamin D, and zinc.

How much to introduce

✳ Begin with one ounce at one meal daily.

✳ Gradually move to two ounces twice daily.

✳ Then two ounces three times daily.

✳ Eventually increase to four ounces per meal.

✳ Your child will dictate how quickly this increases. It is perfectly normal for your baby to eat only between two and four ounces of solids daily while still breast-feeding or formula-feeding, and also for your baby to eat drastically less on some days than others.

What to avoid

✳ Choking hazards—all foods should be puréed until your baby is chewing, at which point all food should be cut into small squares. Always avoid giving your baby nuts, whole grapes, popcorn, chunks of cheese or peanut butter, and candy

✳ Preservatives and salt

✳ Spicy foods

✳ Orange juice and other acidic foods

Nutrition

Just as we have figured out how, where, and when to feed our newborn, she is six months old and we have another question to deal with: What do I feed my baby? Fortunately, while we are learning about our newborn we are given a break, since all she actually needs is milk. Our options for solids can be broken down into the basic food groups: grains, dairy, fruit, vegetables, protein, and oils. These provide humans with all of the nutrients we need, but just how much of each one does your child need every day?

It's a difficult question to answer due to factors such as age, whether she is breast-feeding or formula-feeding, and how much she is taking, and whether or not she has any vitamin deficiencies. I can help you determine your child's food needs depending on age and milk intake; regular checkups with your child's pediatrician should include testing for vitamin deficiencies. Fortunately, all of the necessary nutrients can be found in many different kinds of food, so if your child is allergic to cow's milk, for example, you can purchase alternatives that are enriched with calcium and protein.

The following chart should act as a helpful guide. Bearing in mind that children's dietary preferences and needs vary widely (and let's not forget about picky eaters,) I have focused on providing quantities and food groups rather than proposing specific foods to feed your baby throughout the day. The next three sections of this chapter will give you ideas for choosing and encouraging her to eat specific foods.

The figures given are based on the recommended guidelines of the American Academy of Pediatrics. My figures are not exact but are very close to what they have outlined as daily recommended portions for each of the food groups, depending on a child's age.

6 months old and under

* Mother's milk or formula.

*Around 6 months

* Mother's milk or formula.
* Begin to introduce solids (start with portions as small as ¼ cup of gentle foods such as banana, oatmeal, peaches, pears, squash.)

*Once your breast-fed baby is six months of age, it's important to focus on iron-rich yet age-appropriate foods. A formula-fed baby will continue to receive ample iron but a breast-fed baby will require more than is found in mother's milk. Iron-rich foods include hemp protein, molasses, lentils, prunes, wheat germ, pumpkin, squash seeds, broccoli, nutritional yeast, tofu, and sweet potato.

8 months to one year old

* ½ cup grains.
* ½ cup vegetables.
* Protein by weight (¼ of which can be dairy based.)
* ½ cup fruit.
* 4 cups formula or breast milk.

One year old

* 3 cups milk.
* 1 cup grains.
* 1 cup vegetables.
* Protein by weight.
* 1 cup fruit.
* 2 slices bread.
* 4 tablespoons yogurt or cheese.

Two years old

* 2 ½ cups milk.
* 1 ¼ cup grains.
* 4 tablespoons (¼ cup) vegetables.
* 16 grams protein.
* 2 pieces bread (or 1 ½ plus 4 crackers.)
* ⅔ cup fruit or ½ cup juice or ⅓ cup fruit and 1 cup juice.
* 5 teaspoons of mix of butter, olive oil, salad dressing.

Meal-Plan Template

By now, you've traveled a long way on the food journey—you're expert at two o'clock in the morning feedings; you've witnessed the adorableness that is your child eating watermelon; and you've learned about portions and nutrients. You are ready to delve deeper into a solid-food diet for your child. But it turns out there are even more questions to ask yourself. How can I ensure that my child gets all of the recommended nutrients per day? How can I plan for each day? What if he gets bored with the same foods? I just can't think of anything to feed him today...

Welcome to the world of French fries, food fights, and feelings of failure. You're eating your child's leftovers (macaroni and peas) while anxiously preparing another plate of food for your hungry, cranky child. You have zero confidence that this next plate will be better received. But the truth is that most babies and toddlers are finicky eaters, so don't beat yourself up if your child is not eating everything you make—or even anything you make. You're not a failure and it's not personal. It's not even personal to the food. Some days my daughter loves cucumbers; other days she won't touch them.

I've come up with a meal plan to help you manage all of this. This simple plan is a daily reminder of how much food your child will need each day and what types of food fit into those categories (only write down foods that you know your child will eat.) I keep it on my refrigerator and

refer to it for ideas throughout the day when I'm stumped about what to feed my picky eater. It's also useful to consult while you're making a shopping list. Make sure that you're well stocked up on favorites or anything that your child will eat, including vegetables that may not be favorites but are tolerated. Make this list as long as you can to encourage variety.

Some parents are looking for a meal plan that clearly outlines three meals for each day of the week. This plan is different, and Attachment-Parent friendly, because it is strictly geared toward your child's likes, bringing bonding and harmony at mealtimes. Look at your plan, then make a plate of food with three or four of the foods listed, and there you have it—a kid friendly meal. There's no need for complicated meal planning and it allows you to be extremely flexible with regards to how much time you have to cook that day. If you'd prefer something more structured, with meal content suggested, see the following section on kid friendly meals. It will provide you with many great meal ideas. I have filled in the dietary recommendations for a two-year-old, as an example.

The Template

My child is

> 2 years old

The dietary recommendations for my child are as follows (see the previous section):

> 2 ½ cups of milk
>
> 1 ¼ cup of grains
>
> 4 tablespoons of vegetables (¼ cup)
>
> 16 grams of protein
>
> 2 pieces of bread (or ½ plus 4 crackers)
>
> ⅔ cup of fruit or ½ cup of juice or ⅓ cup of fruit and 1 cup of juice
>
> 5 teaspoons of mix of butter, olive oil, salad dressing

A list of food my child likes (for quick ideas and referencing):

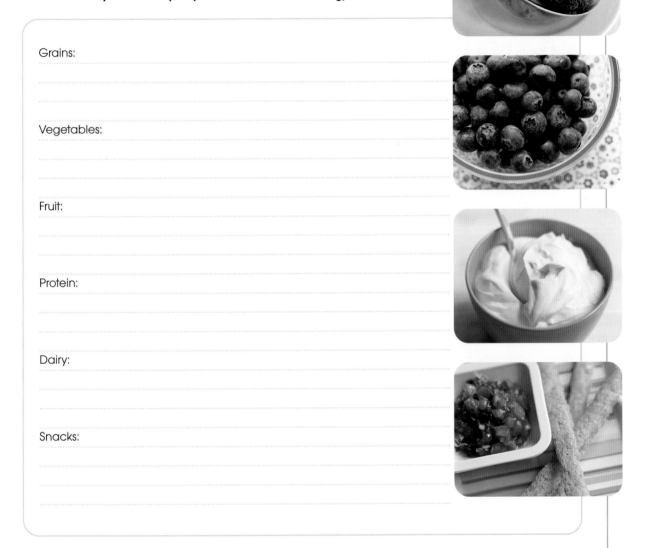

Grains:

Vegetables:

Fruit:

Protein:

Dairy:

Snacks:

My child's specific extra dietary needs and foods that I should be sure to include are: (Asterisk each of the foods you've listed above that meet this dietary requirement as a way to remember to add in these key foods.)

Kid-friendly meals

"Recipes for kids" is a bit of an oxymoron. In my experience, kids don't like foods that are mixed together, unless of course we're talking about cookies and part of that mix is two cups of sugar. Most kids prefer cheese and ketchup to the Thai, Chinese, and Italian flavors found in adult foods. What's more, they rarely tire of their favorite foods and don't realize that certain foods are eaten at certain times of the day. They are at the same time finicky yet fiercely loyal eaters.

When I talk about kid friendly meals, I mean meals that are made up of foods that kids like. I'm sure you have a good idea of your little one's favorite foods and those that will be rejected, but there are probably times when you run out of ideas and feel uninspired. In order to help, I've come up with a list of foods and meal ideas that kids like. They might not all be of the greatest nutritional value, but it's an honest, creative, and practical list that you might find useful.

Some of the ideas listed present a complete meal and others just one food item. It's a very flexible list: the foods listed can be mixed and matched—you can take a snack idea and move it to the lunch section and vice versa. Proteins have been left out because children differ so much on which ones they prefer. Once you've figured it out, add them to any meal accordingly.

Eating can be hard work for kids, so I would like to propose that you choose only one serious meal a day (defined as hot, having to be eaten with a fork, two sides of vegetables, a grain, and a protein.) Your child will welcome the change between lighter, snackier meals and heavier dishes.

Remember to purchase or cook the healthiest version of the ideas presented. French fries should be baked rather than deep-fried; ketchup should be organic rather than the kind with corn syrup listed as the first ingredient; cheeses should be good quality rather than those high in saturated fat; and juice should have no added sugar, and be 100 percent fruit juice.

Breakfast

* Toast topped with jam and side of milk.
* Toast topped with banana, peanut butter, and honey.
* Easy smoothie (banana, orange juice, strawberries, milk.)
* Peanut butter or almond butter smoothie (frozen bananas, milk, butter choice.)
* Pancakes served with side of mango and milk.
* Blueberry muffin and milk.
* Cereal, milk, and side of fruit.
* Hot rice cereal with bananas, milk, and butter (same but with oats and varying fruit.)
* Animal crackers served with fruit and milk.
* Yogurt, fruit, and muffin.
* Apple rings topped with peanut butter and raisins.
* French toast with yogurt and fruit.

Lunch

* Vegetable soup with small pasta shapes mixed in.
* Grilled cheese sandwich with side of broccoli.
* Avocado on toast topped with cucumbers, served with side of pears.
* Bagel or toast with cream cheese topped with cucumber, served with raisins.
* Baked sweet-potato fries served with sautéed zucchini.
* Crackers and almond butter with side of grapes.
* Peanut or almond butter and jam sandwich with side of milk.
* Quesadilla, side of raw carrots, and dip (white bean, hummus, or creamy zucchini dip.)
* Nachos (baked tortilla chips, cheddar cheese, and any toppings your child likes.)

Dinner

✳ Baked French fries topped with cheddar cheese and a side of steamed baby carrots.

✳ Penne cooked and cut into ⅛-inch rings. Mix marinara and mozzarella together for a sauce and serve with side of steamed zucchini.

✳ Elbow pasta with homemade cheese sauce (milk, butter, cheddar). Serve peas topped with light butter and salt on the side.

✳ English muffins topped with tomato sauce, mozzarella, and your child's favorite topping.

✳ Chinese fried rice (white rice, peas, carrots, very fine cabbage, in light Chinese sauce.)

✳ Black-bean burgers served with mashed potatoes and steamed carrots.

✳ White rice with crushed almonds mixed in, served with a side of chickpea and cucumber salad with vinaigrette dressing.

✳ Broccoli, cheese, and almond meal fritters served with a side of butternut squash.

Vegetables

Sweet potato, peas, winter sweet squashes, carrots, broccoli, cucumber, zucchini, yellow squash, and cauliflower are all kid friendly

vegetables. I know your child will not like all of these but try to get her used to at least a few. Keli appreciates vegetables best when they've been prepared in butter with light salt.

Snacks

* Granola bar
* Sorbet
* Fruit bar
* Green smoothie
* Muffin
* Yogurt with bananas and animal crackers.
* Banana coated in peanut butter rolled in rice cereal.
* Cucumbers and lightly steamed baby carrots with hummus dip.
* Pretzels served with hummus or melted cheddar-cheese dip.
* Rice cakes topped with peanut butter and honey or cheese spread.
* Chips dipped in avocado, chip dip, cream cheese, or hummus.
* Toast served with applesauce and milk.

Your Picky Eater

If you are the parent of a finicky eater then you know that some days he really won't eat anything, and that some days can turn into two or three days. If your child receives regular health checkups and is at a healthy weight then try to relax. This is normal toddler behavior; you and your little one will survive this phase. Try implementing the first five tricks below to encourage balanced meal eating. If your child is resisting and you are desperate to get him to eat anything, tips five through ten should be helpful.

3 **Choose the lesser evil.** Babies do really well with distraction at mealtime. It prevents them from playing with their food or becoming bored with sitting too long, which can result in aversion to mealtimes. You could let him watch an educational video, but make sure that whatever you choose is not overly distracting. When he gets older you can bribe him: "If you eat your broccoli, you can have a candy bean after dinner."

1 **Eat with your child.** Kids want to do what mommy and daddy are doing. Most likely he will be eating something different but he will enjoy the mealtime environment you've created. Your toddler may want to eat from your plate; that's a great way of introducing him to new foods.

4 **Learn what your child likes.** Start introducing healthy foods and see which ones your toddler likes best. Patterns will develop. Dislikes will be obvious, but you'll also notice that he becomes excited about certain foods and never turns those down.

2 **Serve it the way he prefers it.** Some children will prefer a bowl and spoon while others will eat better if their food is separated on a plate and handed to them with a fork. Be sure to offer a cup of water and to make sure the food isn't too hot. Also, many kids eat more when their food is brought to them one course at a time.

5 **Make a "you can spit it out if you don't like it rule."** Most of us are familiar with the rule that works best for parents: "You have to at least try it." But perhaps we don't always follow up with a very clear: "You can spit it out if you don't like it." Be sure he knows that it's okay to ask for something different and that you are happy to remove a food that has been tried and not liked.

6 **Serve fruit and milk for breakfast, vegetables for lunch, grains and protein for dinner.** If your child hasn't eaten for a day or more, you may want to focus on one food group per meal as a way of getting a mix of nutrients in for the day. A lot of kids eat better with just one type of food in front of them and only one course as a single serving of food doesn't overwhelm them.

7 **If all else fails, anything will do!** If Keli hadn't eaten anything for a whole day and had refused all the healthy, nutritious options that I had offered, the goal became to get her to eat anything at all. At this point, it is very much okay to make macaroni and cheese, rice and butter, or a muffin (something rich in calories and filling.) Focus less on giving your child a well-balanced meal if it will assist you in getting calories into her.

8 **Breast milk and toddler milk.** If your child is still drinking either of these, don't worry too much about nutrition. Both breast milk and toddler milk provide a finicky eater with most of the nutrients he needs. If you can, I recommend offering either of these to a child who is not eating well.

9 **Make smoothies.** If your child will drink them, smoothies are a great solution to feeding the finicky eater. Make them from whatever your child needs the most. Bananas are a nice base because they are filling and naturally sweet. You can add greens, more fruit, milk, juice, a vitamin. Smoothies are filling and delicious and best of all, to your fussy child they are not food.

10 **Give your child a multivitamin.** In order to do this, you may have to sneak the vitamin into a rather sugary drink. Most kids love very sweet juice, and liquid kid's vitamins are mildly sweet and so are well disguised in juice or a smoothie. Consult your pediatrician for recommendations and doses.

CHAPTER 5:
Toddler Tips

Highly-Sensitive Toddlers

It was no surprise to us when our high-need baby became a highly-sensitive toddler. A sensitive person has a highly aware nervous system, causing quick reactions to everything, and we had seen plenty of this well before Keli was a toddler. Many of the traits that commonly define highly-sensitive children develop as your child's personality develops, so it can be hard to identify whether or not you have a highly sensitive child before she is one.

What are the signs that a toddler is highly sensitive?

There are many behavioral signs that demonstrate that your toddler is highly sensitive. She may be demanding, clingy, easily overstimulated, and cautious. You may also notice that she doesn't adjust well to new situations and new people, and she may be fearful, empathetic, and intense. Highly-sensitive toddlers are usually clever for their age and have an advanced vocabulary. Many highly-sensitive children don't unwind easily at night, are perfectionists, and are sensitive to taste, touch, and smell.

Although some of these traits are challenging, they are in fact amazing when you consider the emotional depth necessary for your child to experience her world in this way. Parenting a highly- sensitive toddler can be exhausting, but it will also bring you joy as your child deciphers her world in an inquisitive, loving, and fully present way. Life with Keli has been a paradox. She can be an incredible handful, but she makes me smile more times in a day than I can count.

The followings tips are designed to help you and your highly-sensitive (HS) toddler. You will find advice on preventing and handling toddler tantrums that applies to all toddlers in the section that follows (Preventing Toddler Tantrums, pages 106–109.) Naturally, there will be overlaps, but there are key differences to be taken into account when parenting a highly-sensitive toddler. The tips that follow were created with those differences in mind.

Ways to Help You and Your HS Toddler

1 **Be positive.** Highly-sensitive children experience intense emotional feelings. Whether you are reprimanding your little one or trying to understand what a tantrum is about, it is important to be patient, calm, reassuring, and helpful.

3 **Provide choices.** Sensitive children are highly aware and more likely to become frustrated or feel hurt by a loss of power. When you give a child a choice, she feels respected; this is especially important to your little one. As with all toddlers, give a limited number of reasonable choices.

2 **Give positive reinforcement.** Sensitive children feel things deeply and are likely to take everyday conflicts to heart. Be sure that your child feels loved, happy, confident, and smart. If she knows that the relationship you share is based on unconditional acceptance, it will be easier for her to accept correction and boundaries.

4 **Provide consistent routines.** Highly sensitive children feel more peaceful and secure when they have a sense of control. Having a daily routine wil help your child to stay calm; she will know what to expect and will not be distracted by or anxious of the unknown.

5 **Avoid saying "no."** A firm "no" will all but beg a defensive, sad, ashamed, startled, or misunderstood reaction from your child. It is better to redirect a highly sensitive child. Instead of saying, "No hands in the ketchup," try, "Just one finger in the ketchup" or "Just French fries go in the ketchup." You can always change a negative comment into a positive.

6 **Teach the importance of practice.**
I praise practice as much as accomplishment. Studies show that this attitude encourages your child to spend more time trying to work through tasks. For example, "You haven't learned to pour juice yet but you do a great job drinking out of a big-kid cup. You practiced and you got better. I'm most proud of you when you practice." This is helpful to highly-sensitive children because they are often perfectionists who can become easily discouraged.

7 **Prepare your child for the day's events.**
You can reduce conflict and anxiety by discussing the day's plans with your child ahead of time. This might include mentioning any big outings, visitors, and when mommy may be busy. If you're going somewhere new, outline rules and expectations. HS children respond well to being trusted within boundaries that a parent has set lovingly.

8 **Don't rush your child.** A busy day makes everyone feel stressed and this is especially true for your little one. If you know you're going to have a busy day, don't forget to schedule in time to connect with and support your child. It will most likely end up saving you time. Try not to push your child out the door if you have to go somewhere. Give her plenty of time for eating, getting dressed, and transitioning from one activity to the next.

9 **Time transition times.** Your toddler may struggle with daily transitions between activities. Help by saying to her before leaving the house, for example, "We're leaving in ten minutes," then, "In five minutes" and, "Two more minutes!" If you haven't already done so, transition times are a good opportunity to talk about plans and expectations as your HS one may feel anxious about whatever is coming next.

10 **If your child resists a new activity, let it go.** Ask her if she wants to do something, let her know you'll be right there, encourage her, and try to remove the fear from the situation, but if none of that works, let it go. Beyond your encouragement and support, it's best to leave the decision about trying something new to your little one.

11 **Be brave.** Even though your child may not like newness, especially new outings, try them a few times before giving up. Keep in mind that HS children can take an hour to adjust to a new setting or may need to visit a place a few times before enjoying it. Try not to believe that something that's difficult will therefore not be worth it. Some of a child's best adventures will be ones she had to warm up to first.

13 **During a meltdown or tantrum, nurture your child.** HS children have to be soothed and helped out of their intense emotional state before you can rationalize with them. Once your child is calm, ask her what happened, how she may have handled things differently, or what you can do to help.

12 **Create a nest, a safe place.** Most of us know when a meltdown is coming. If your child is having a particularly rough day, she may be tired, but if she is HS it could be that she's feeling overwhelmed or overstimulated. We like to take Keli to a soothing place with dim lights, calm music, and comfortable nesting. It helps her to recharge and can turn a bad day into a better one.

14 **Validate your child's concern.** HS children need to know they are understood. Simply repeating back to your child the cause of her upset may calm her down quickly. For example, if she says "My leg hurts, my leg hurts, my leg hurts," she needs you to give these words back to her and show that you understand. Saying "Your leg hurts. I know your leg hurts" should provide the reassurance she needs.

15 **Countdown to calm down.** When nothing I say helps to calm my daughter down, I can almost see the expression on her face that means, "Save me." She knows she's overreacting but can't help it. I'll say, "Mommy is going to count to five and then you can calm down." She agrees and, as I count, she has taught herself to take deep breaths and is calm by five. Sometimes, she even asks me to do it: "Momma, count to five and baby calm down." Once she's calm, I hug her, kiss her, and we talk about it.

16 **Follow the golden distraction rule.** Generally, I don't recommend distraction with older children, but I think it's more beneficial than harmful for our HS little ones. Avoiding emotional meltdowns will spare them a great deal. Nip meltdowns in the bud by distracting your child. You might quickly point out a dog being walked, a squirrel in your yard, or ask if they'd like a yummy snack. You might need to move your child into another room and involve her in a new activity to make sure that the previous situation is out of sight and mind. When your child is older, you can be more transparent about doing this. For example, I might say to Keli, "This toy keeps making you cry. I think we should put it away so it won't make you cry and then we can go to the kitchen for a snack." She usually consents with relief.

17 **Be calm before handling conflicts.** Your highly-sensitive child will know if you are upset or stressed and will mirror your emotions. Take deep breaths for ten seconds and tell yourself, "Wow, she's really worked up, poor thing. I need to calm her down." Proceed with level-headedness and understanding. It's not easy to calm yourself down. Take up the habit of venting to your partner later about the moments when you felt frustrated but couldn't show it.

18 **Have boundaries.** It might sound as if I'm suggesting that you be super-easy on your highly-sensitive child. This approach can work but you should also have boundaries and be consistent. Spirited toddlers will test you repeatedly and they need consistency more than anyone else. They will trust you to guide and help them when they are out of control. If you are inconsistent, your child will be confused about what is and isn't okay.

19 **Appreciate your child's wonderful traits.** Whether disciplining, reading stories together, or going to a new place, be aware of her sensitivity. All children thrive when their uniqueness is understood, accepted, and nurtured. Take it further by cultivating her positive traits such as empathy, intuitiveness, and curiosity.

Preventing Toddler Tantrums: The Loving Psychology Behind It All

There are two underlying causes of the discontentment behind your toddler's tantrums:

* Your child feels powerless; he feels helpless, disrespected, and is unable to express his emotions adequately, resulting in frustration.
* Your child wants more attention and feels angry and hurt that he is not receiving it.

A toddler naturally feels frustrated by being constantly told what to do. Most tantrums are caused by your child's built-up frustration and actually have little to do with the object or activity that he cannot have in the moment. The strategies offered below can be implemented easily and will help you to reduce your little one's frustration while providing more opportunities to connect in a day.

Teach your child how to express his feelings

If your child knows how to share his feelings in a productive way, he may rely on using words rather than lashing out. Lashing out can be done for attention; however, it can also occur simply because a child is not equipped to handle the emotion in any other way. If your child can label those negative emotions, he can ask for your help with them.

When reading books together, talk about the characters' feelings. For example, ask your child, "How is that bear feeling now?" or "What kind of face does that little girl have?" Children can learn to read emotions at a very early age and you'll notice that they take great interest in understanding facial expressions. Make happy and mad faces with your

child. Talk about what makes him happy, mad, and sad and then talk about what makes mommy grouchy, excited, or upset. Sentences such as, "I can see that you are mad right now" are very important and give your child the words he needs when feeling upset.

Respect your child

Many tantrums are due to your child's frustration with not being understood and feeling as though he has no control over his life. If you can find little ways to show him that he's respected and trusted to make decisions, he will be happier. You'll notice a huge decrease in the number of tantrums. There are many ways to show your toddler that you respect him. Here are just three:

Teach natural consequences over punishment

Teach your child that the world is full of consequences that mommy and daddy do not control. Explain these consequences simply, but be sure your child understands the natural consequences of his behavior. For example, one night Keli wanted to play with her Kindle instead of reading (something I very rarely allow.) At lights-out time she decided she wanted to read. She cried a bit when I explained to her how her decision to play with the Kindle had affected reading time and then she accepted it. Teaching natural consequences helps your child to develop good judgment rather than blind obedience and will benefit him in the long term.

Provide routine and give your child choices

Routine gives children both a feeling of knowing what's going on and their own sense of time, both of which are important factors in feeling in control. Giving your child choices throughout the day gives him a sense that he has some say about his environment and that you value his opinion on things. This will make him feel more helpful and empowered. Of course, you cannot always give your child a choice but many situations arise where you can. For example: what shoes to wear, where to go first, grapes or apple, red construction paper or blue, and so on.

Let your child believe that you are equals

Pretend that he is helping you do something that you could not manage by yourself. Keli likes to pretend that her dolls need her to help do things. She relishes the phrase: "My baby needs me to teach her how." She enjoys helping me while I pretend that my hands are full and I truly need her. She'll even say, "Oh, mommy's hands are so full" in a way that shows she's gaining real pleasure from helping and believing that she is truly needed. Similarly, she likes it when I'm wrong, so we will sing songs incorrectly or pretend that we cannot find something that is close by so that Keli can correct us and save the day.

Be sure your child feels your love no matter how busy you are

Your child wants your attention much more than it is humanly possible to give it. This imbalance becomes a real problem when he feels that you are always preoccupied. Whenever possible, play with your child; I can't say that enough. Try to sit down two to three times daily for fully devoted hour-long play sessions. Try never to ignore your child's questions and always answer if he asks you to play or to come and see something that he has done. You may not be able to do what he wants at that moment, but you can acknowledge or praise what he is doing.

Listen to your child with real interest. Children know when they are being brushed off. If you are very busy one day, give your child hugs throughout the day and remind him that tomorrow you'll do something special together.

Prepare your toddler for any upcoming event that is likely to cause tantrums

If you are going to do something that irritates your child then he will try to annoy you while you're doing it. It's a law of physics. If you need to cook dinner, check your email, or make a business phone call, find something exciting for your child to do while you're busy. There's no point to starting a task that will end in frustration for both of you—and you're all too aware what your child's triggers are. Sometimes we forget that we have no right to do as we please. Remember to consider your toddler before doing anything. Busy boxes are a great idea for these situations (see page 122.)

There's a less tangible form of preparation reserved for out-of-the-house activities. If you have a busy day planned, talk to your child well beforehand about what's going to happen next. If you're going grocery shopping, remind him of the rules ahead of time. Rather than being negative about the situation, you might get him excited instead. Here are some examples of questions you could ask him before going out: "We're going to the grocery store after your nap. What will we do there? Should you run or not run in the store? You can stay in the cart for a ride but how about you come out to help me put the

vegetables in the bags?" In this way your child won't be taken aback by your expectations once you get there, and you have leverage too: "Remember we said you could come out of the cart once we are buying vegetables?" Of course, you will buy the vegetables last. This also works for trips to restaurants, the toy store, and grandma's house.

Improve connection via daily affirmation

Your toddler will feel like he needs your help too often. By giving him positive reinforcement throughout the day you give him the confidence that he can do some things wonderfully on his own. This will instill independence in the long term and in the short term make your child's day a little more pleasant. I like to give Keli high-fives when she does something great. I also make up songs where she is the main character and the song's lyrics describe all the things I love about her or the details of what she has accomplished that day.

Calm an over- or under-stimulated child

Many parents notice that their child is not having a great day long before the tantrums begin. Whatever the reason for your child having a bad day, this calls for what I term a "recharge." If your child seems miserable, change his environment. The great outdoors often does the trick if a child is bored, but you can also create a quiet nest in your home where you can sit, read books together, and regroup should your child be over-stimulated. This area should be dim, have comfy seating, and maybe calm music.

Create an environment that is really kid friendly

The more kid friendly your living space is, the less often you will have to say, "No." What could be simpler at preventing tantrums than that? Put glass decorations and other dangerous household items away and make it easier for your child to reach the things he wants to play with. When considering the interior design of your home, ask yourself, "How can I make this place more fun, accessible, and safe for my child?" This will help you to design an accessible play area (see pages 120–125 for tips.)

Don't rush your toddler into things

This will cause unnecessary stress and may even damage your toddler's self-esteem as he may feel that he cannot keep up the pace and is disappointing you. Being parents, we have developed all sorts of techniques for getting our little one out of the door quickly, but hurrying a small person who has no concept of time, schedules, meetings, or closing times can create tension.

Managing Toddler Tantrums

No matter how much prevention you implement, there will come a day when your child begins to say "no" to you. This is cute at first. As proud parents, we see this as a development in language and a step toward independence. Unfortunately "no" is soon accompanied by the frustrated stomping and angry screaming of a toddler tantrum. These are rarely proud moments for parent or child, but both can learn a great deal from them.

Even when you're not going to give your toddler what she is asking for, you can sympathize. It's important to work with your child rather than against her while handling tantrums. As parents, we may wonder how a little person can be so terribly upset over the smallest things, but in fact, as explained in the previous section, she is upset about the bigger picture: the way in which you are responding to her feelings.

Your child might try to manipulate your sympathy but by staying sympathetic to him while remaining fixed in your boundaries, your child will develop respect for your approach to handling conflicts. You can learn about

your child's needs and communication limits; she can learn about your unconditional love and boundaries.

The following steps pave the way toward effective and loving behavior management.

Acknowledge your child's feelings

Children will often stop a tantrum as soon as they realize that you understand and sympathize with them. You might say, "I know you are sad about bedtime. I'm very sorry. All little kids don't like bedtime. It makes them sad!" This has worked wonders for us. Avoid getting into a mindset where the goal is to make your child stop crying. Instead, think of tantrums as an opportunity to learn about what bothers her and why. Followed up with compassion and education about why we can't always have what we want. This might quiet your child's cries even if you don't do it with the no-cry goal in mind.

Use simple, short sentences

Toddlers can handle only so much information at one time; once they are upset this threshold decreases drastically. When you are reminding a child of a rule, a simple, "Hands are not for hitting with" or "Chairs are not for standing on" will do the trick. You can explain your reasons, but keep them short and sweet, and only when she has stopped the tantrum, for example, "If you stand on chairs, you could fall and get hurt." Avoid expressing anger, frustration, or worry. You are likely to be feeling more emotion than your child has the capacity to understand; toddlers should not be an outlet for that.

Remember to stay calm

This may sound more like a Buddhist practice than an everyday parenting skill and remembering to stay

calm is not a once-you-get-it-you've-got-it skill. This takes awareness and discipline. If you remember to act calmly, you will get through to your toddler during tantrums more effectively than by displaying anger or anxiety. Notice that I said "act" calmly. You may have to pretend to be calm. Take a few deep breaths and feign composure. After doing this for a few weeks, you may even find that you really do become calmer during conflicts.

Do not resort to name calling

You may be thinking that you would never do that but uttering phrases such as, "You're bad," "You are so stubborn," or "Why can't you eat without making a mess?" is name calling. Without realizing it, parents tend to shame their children into doing what they want. Using negative attributes to describe your child will adversely affect her self-esteem and won't help you to accomplish your goal of ending a tantrum. She needs to know that spilling milk on peas is naughty, not that she is naughty. Your job is to teach your child good from bad actions, without describing her personality as one of these in the process.

Whenever possible, ignore bad behavior

It's better to say "no" calmly and move a child away from what she is doing, even if you have to move her ten times, than to give her a harsh demand that makes her stop immediately. This is only going to upset you both by creating a "you-against-me" moment. If your child is seeking attention, then you are likely rewarding her when you get worked up about her behavior. The first few times you adopt this approach, your child will probably return to the undesirable action, but eventually she will realize that this behavior will have to stop and that you will not put on a show about it.

Negotiate

A toddler naturally feels frustrated because they are always the one that has to surrender, so you might strike a deal at times: " If you want to play with your blocks for a while longer, we'll only read two books tonight," or "If you can wait patiently while I shop, I'll buy you a treat." Some people might think these are bribes but I think a better way of seeing it is that you both win. Your child doesn't have to know that her win is smaller than yours.

Be compassionate

Cultivate a compassionate state of mind. You are your child's best, if not only, ally. When your child is upset about something, tell her it upsets you too. When it's something that is completely out of your hands, explain to your child that you also would like the outcome to be different (i.e. if the toy store is closed, explain to your child that you wish the store had been open.) Try not to dismiss your child in an annoyed or impatient way. She may be crying or whining about something that cannot be changed but allow her to express her frustration anyway. Think about how you feel when you've been deeply let down and how you would like to be spoken to.

Develop a consistent warning system

I like to give Keli the "5,4,3,2,1..." warning. Any timing system will be more respected by your toddler if you sometimes use it in her favor. You don't often hear, "5,4,3,2,1, ice-cream time!" but why not? The important thing is that when you are counting down and get to zero, you are consistent and always do as you said you would.

Use a timer whenever possible

Your child is probably under the impression that you are the rule-maker and this creates tension in your relationship. You can remove some of this tension by using a kitchen timer as another authority symbol. A timer can be used at the park, for example: "When the timer goes off in five minutes, it's time to go home." I have found that it's important to use the timer to indicate positive results as well. Your child will develop more respect for the timer if it sometimes plays a positive role in her life.

Make an effort to understand the underlying cause of your child's unwanted behaviors

If you often find yourself in a parent-toddler power struggle, you are probably familiar with the following phrases: "No!", "This is mine!", "I don't want to take a bath!" It's likely that your responses often sound similar: "Don't say no to mommy," "This is not yours, you have to share it," "You're dirty so you have to take a bath." While none of these are necessarily unkind responses they are unhelpful at limiting tantrums. Figure out why your child doesn't want to share her toy or take a bath and then encourage problem solving. It may be that she's just feeling argumentative but oftentimes there will be more to it.

Timeouts

There will come a time, every now and then, when nothing you do or say will stop your child from acting out. I can honestly say that we have yet to see such a time from our child, and I believe that is because we practice all of these tips. I would reserve timeouts for those times when all else fails and advise against using them for everyday toddler naughtiness. When a child refuses get off the table, continues to misuse a household item, and follows such actions with screaming and kicking, you may need to enforce a timeout. Please try everything else in this chapter first. If nothing works, your child may well be sending you the message, "Your old tricks aren't going to work!" If she is showing this kind of stubbornness, it may be time calmly to go with her to your timeout spot. You will sit together until the tantrum has ended, at which point you may go back to playing. Once she is calm, talk about why she was sent to timeout.

Don't be intimidated by your toddler

Some parents are content to be harsh and take the quickest possible route to ending a tantrum. They are setting themselves up for years of unproductive parent–child conflict. Other parents are patient and kind but afraid of implementing new methods or approaches to minimize the frequency and intensity of tantrums, thinking that their child's fit may escalate. Your toddler, no matter how serious and in charge she may seem to be at times is just that: a toddler. She is completely out of control and needs you. Do not be intimidated by her behavior, no matter how intense it becomes. Your helpless child is underneath there and is in need of mommy or daddy's assistance.

Top Tips for Toddler Tantrums

Keli began to throw mini-tantrums when she was a little under the age of one. She started with "No!" around eleven months. The reasons for this were things such as not wanting to wear her shoes, have her diaper changed, or her hair brushed. She'd throw tantrums about having to sit in her stroller or get dressed. These are all pretty normal reasons for toddlers to throw tantrums. In fact, tantrums start as such irrational little fits that I don't think much qualifies as an abnormal reason to throw one. With Keli, we developed many save-the-day strategies while in the thick of these tantrums.

Children have tantrums about things in phases and outgrow certain aversions very quickly. There are a few on the list, however, that seem immortal. If the phrases, "You have to finish your dinner," "You know you have to take a bath," and "If we don't brush your teeth you're going to get cavities" are painfully familiar to you, see below for ideas on how to respond.

"I don't want to eat"

* "I don't want to eat" is often code for "I'm too busy having fun." What can you do but to compete with the fun? I recommend making mealtimes more entertaining for your child: eat with him, put on an educational video, play a word game together such as "I spy," or put on a puppet show. The key is to notice whether this is keeping your child seated and eating or is overly distracting. Scale back on the entertainment if necessary.

* If you're serving two or more different foods for your child's meal, bring them out one at a time. This will help him to focus on the simple task of eating this one food. Children can become overwhelmed by too many choices and begin to play with their food or accidentally mix it together. It's also likely that one undesirable food item on his plate will ruin the whole meal.

* Experiment with new foods but not too often. It's important to know what your child likes to eat and to serve that food. You will of course experiment with new foods in order to broaden his horizons, but consider saving those for snack times or as an extra, alternative course to a meal just in case it doesn't go well. You'll be most successful once you've discovered a handful of foods that are almost always winners with your child.

"No, I don't need a bath"

* "I don't need a bath" is not code for anything really. It's true: your little one does not have to take a bath. But you would prefer it if he was clean, so you're going to have to entertain him. I recommend filling the bathtub with toys; not just rubber ducks but some of the new state-of-the-art tub toys on the market. Then there are classics such as fish and fishnet, bubbles, and bathtub crayons. Keli used to enjoy washing her sea animals with a washcloth and then it would be her turn to get washed. Bath time will require variety so have enough toys on hand that you can mix them up from time to time.

* Consider your little one's bath-time discomforts, such as uncomfortable water temperature, getting water in the eyes, having to stay in longer than he'd like, or being washed by someone else. None of these things would be any more welcomed by ourselves. Be sure that the water is

just right, purchase a shampoo guard for hair washing, and be generally considerate in your role as bath giver.

✳ Hide the washcloths, shampoos, and soaps so that he will want to get into the bath to play. Let him play before he gets washed because many toddlers will end up crying and want to get straight out after having their hair washed, reinforcing the fact that bath time is not fun. Begin with fun and wait to wash until the last minute, making it a quick event. If you trust him to do the body washing, even better.

"I don't want to brush my teeth"

✳ This is most definitely code for "I don't realize how much more terrible sitting in a dentist chair while getting a cavity filled would be." I recommend telling your little one all about cavities. Watch some educational videos and allow him to have a healthy fear of bad oral hygiene.

✳ Make teeth brushing more fun. Sing a song while you brush your toddler's teeth—ours was "Chugga Chugga Brush Brush." Let your child have a turn. Have him choose his own toothbrush and nice flavored tooth paste, and allow him to brush your teeth; or play dentist, where you say, "Hello, I'm dentist. What's your name, what have you eaten today? I see that you had some sugar right here, and there's a big pumpkin over there that I have to get out!" Follow up with compliments about how often he must be brushing. Keep the games coming and be cheerful. If your child has let you in there, he deserves your undivided showman skills.

✳ If you've tried all things creative, count down as you brush. Have your little one brush by himself for as long as he'd like and then tell him you're going to brush his teeth for ten seconds. Count down slowly and brush as well as you can. Just knowing there's an end in sight should calm your little one when it's time to open up for those "ahhhs" and "eees."

Traveling with Your Toddler

Keli is now three years old. We've visited family out of state six times. In anticipation of each flight, I delved deep into thinking about the inevitable pending disaster and how to avoid it. I spent time researching tips and preparing as much as possible, with Keli's needs at the center of all of my considerations. At first, I was surprised when our adventures went well. They went better than well: she did great. Now I expect her to do well. Below is a list of tips specific to traveling with a toddler, but many of them would also work for a younger baby.

2 **Have at least three brand new toys for the plane.** As soon as your little one starts to get antsy, give her a toy; to get the maximum usage out of each one, don't give her all of them at once. You might even consider getting three new toys for the return journey. Small but interesting toys are best. In the past, we've bought oversized magnets, wipe-off books, and other lap-intended doodling boards. Stickers, blue painters' tape, and low-mess sculpting material are great, too.

3 **Don't forget to bring some of your little one's favorite toys too.** This is both for when you get to where you're going (so she feels at home) and also because favorites are always good.

1 **If you nurse your child, bring a comfortable cover-up blouse of some sort.** It is often hot on a plane, so I recommend a light cover-up, but sometimes, once off the ground, it can get cold. You may consider taking a cover-up and a blanket.

4 **Pack candy.** There's nothing wrong with a lollipop, jellybean, or small piece of chocolate if it will save your trip. Even if it doesn't save your trip, I can promise you that it will at least divert a crisis or two.

5 **Make friends while you wait to board your plane and everyone will think your child is cute and loveable.** Take advantage of this grace period. You'll feel better boarding if you know that the people on the plane don't already think of your child as a nap-interrupting demon.

6 **Sit near the aisle if possible.** You may think it would be best to contain your little one in a window seat. There's some truth to this because if your child is shy it will give her some privacy as well as a view that might be entertaining. However, most children will want to explore and need the option to get up once or twice during the flight. Also, don't hesitate (if there are empty seats on the plane) to talk to the flight attendant about moving where you won't have a neighbor.

7 **Make sure your child is changed, fed, and tired when you get on the plane.** Tired? Yes. This is the one time that having her rested is not a prerequisite for the upcoming adventure. You want your child to sleep on the plane.

8 **If you have a toy or computer that shows movies or plays apps,** download new stuff before you go and bring it out whenever necessary for hours of entertainment. Don't think about this not being good for your child. What's not good for your child is being bored to tears, antsy, needing to move, or anxious.

9 **Pack mess-free snacks.** Pack snacks that your child will think of as treats. Kids love treats and will sit quietly and happily eating them. Mess-free treats include a granola bar, dry cereal, cheese crackers, chips, and fruit snacks.

10 **Layovers are no longer your enemy, so consider purchasing a one-stop flight.** Layovers might as well be called lifesavers—not only will they help you save a little cash, seeing as you are now paying an extra three-hundred dollars to fly your child, but they will also give her a chance to run around, eat something, scream, break something, and then (maybe) finish the trip feeling a bit more relaxed.

CHAPTER 6:

Entertaining and Educating Your Child

Your 6–10 Month Old

Until recently, your baby hasn't shown much interest in playing, or if he has, he hasn't yet developed the necessary skills to play. Mastering sitting up and crawling have probably been occupying his attention. Before six months, most babies have an array of toys surrounding the play area and the two of you will have spent most playtimes shaking a toy together, encouraging movement, or playing tickling games.

Sometime near the six-month mark, playtime changes. Soon, your child will be crawling and showing less interest in rattles and mirror-covered noisy books. Now, he'll want to make more of his fun surroundings and will seek your guidance as he explores exciting new toys, as well as household items. It's time to step outside of your supervising role and move into the role of baby entertainer.

To prepare you for this, I've suggested some age-appropriate play ideas. The key here is "age appropriate." At 6–10 months old, your child's hand-eye coordination and gross motor skills are still developing. Play at this age will largely require simple toys and parent-led activities.

Play ideas for this age group

✳ Place your largest pot or bucket in the bathtub and fill it with cups, ladles, and scoops. Although it may seem to make sense to fill your bathtub, there is something more appealing to your child about playing in a bucket of water.

✳ Educational videos such as *Baby Genius* and *Baby Einstein*.

✳ Sit down with a basket of toys. Take one toy out at a time and play with it. Your child will notice and will join you to play with toys that otherwise might go unnoticed or unappreciated. A strange but true law of kid play is that your showing something makes it more appealing.

✳ Make one kitchen cabinet your child's. This should be within his reach and filled with various kitchen supplies. This will keep him entertained while you're cooking.

✳ Read books together.

✳ Talk or read books using puppets to help tell the story.

✳ Take your child on a magic blanket ride. Have him sit on one end of an opened-up throw blanket, grab the other end, and pull him around the house for a ride.

✳ Give him flashcard lessons.

✳ If you have a chair that spins or rocks, give your baby a fun chair ride.

✳ Lean a cookie sheet against your couch to the floor at an angle. Give your little one blocks, cars, or balls to slide down it.

✳ Set a time for singing songs and doing finger-play.

✳ Build towers with blocks.

✳ Music time: Pull out a box of musical instruments to play together.

✳ Create a fun-bin: This is a bin of various toys or household items that change weekly. Keep it

fresh and allow your child to explore it daily.

✳ School time: I recommend teaching animal names and sounds, the names of household items, and basic language such as "yes, no, tired, and hungry." Puzzles, colored flash cards, and texture books are great for this age group.

Toys

Young babies will enjoy playing with blocks, stacking buckets, balls, dolls, cars, puppets, chunky puzzles, and musical instruments. They will also like talking books and a few (truly limited) larger plastic toys, such as a playhouse or talking animal toy. These types of toys often mimic each other and quickly become boring so focus on finding good-quality ones and switch them once the novelty wears off.

Your 10–18 Month Old

At around ten months old, babies develop an incredible amount of character and an interest in what adults are doing. Your child is mostly likely standing and so getting into everything. Her intelligence and need for stimulation have increased. She is active, clingy, and easily bored. This is a really difficult time to be a stay-at-home mother or father (for advice and tips on coping as a stay-at-home parent, please see the following chapter.)

Fortunately, as your child's need for entertainment increases, her play skills advance. Around this time, you can introduce an art session to your child's day. You will also notice that she enjoys imitating you. It will be very basic, but imaginative play begins now (reflected in the ideas below.) Keeping this age group entertained and stimulated requires more energy and planning but once your child is engaged in these fun activities, she will show some independence. For the first time, you'll be able to sit back and just watch.

Play ideas for this age group

* Make four or more busy boxes: These are small boxes containing the contents for one activity in them, all set up and ready to go. These remain a novelty because they are not left out with her other toys but pulled out when you need your child to be entertained for a moment. Things to include could be contents for a craft, a pouring activity, a magnet box, supplies for a gluing activity, clay and clay tools, etc.
* Take every pillow in your home and make a pillow pile. Let the jumping and climbing begin.
* Purchase or make a sandbox. Be sure to add sand toys.
* Try blowing bubbles and hula-hooping at the same time.
* Play at cleaning together. Be sure your child has her own kid cleaning supplies.
* A play kitchen is a great toy for your newly standing baby. She will enjoy pretending to cook or wash the dishes. Play kitchens can be expensive but it is a toy that will last well until your child's seventh birthday.
* Purchase educational game apps for your phone or tablet.
* Have a snack and story time in a play tent.
* Have a dance party.
* Collect and explore nature items.
* Fill a bucket with differently colored buttons, pom-poms, play coins, and beads. Take out an

ice tray and encourage your child to sort by color, shape, or material.

* Sensory table: Fill a sand or water table with sensory items and supplies such as empty water bottles, funnels, scoops, ice trays, tongs, fishnet, and play animals. These will always be accessible to your child as she explores each new sensory theme. It's key to change the sensory table at least once a week. Ideas for its contents include: pasta, rice, beans, dyed-blue pasta for water, cotton for snow, confetti, plastic Easter eggs hidden under colored feathers and filled with small treasures, hidden items in pieces of cut-up tissue paper. I recommend searching the Internet for creative and fun themes. (This was Keli's number one source of entertainment for a solid six months.)

* Cut out felt handprints and footprints in different colors. Tape them to the floor and have your toddler jump on the footprints, placing her hands down where she sees a handprint. She will love this colorful and playful activity, jumping around the room.

* Set up a play picnic: Lay out a big blanket and set up a play activity of any sort (for example, coloring books, blocks, toy picnic, musical instruments.) I don't understand the secret to it, but your child will be drawn to this play picnic as if it were magical.

* Create a nature map: Draw a nature scene on a large poster board complete with a jungle, barn, pond, ocean, and trees. Take out your child's play animals and nature basket and have her bring the map to life by placing animals where they live and decorating the habitats with items from the nature basket, such as leaves, rocks, and pinecones.

* Roughhouse with your child: Spin, lift, tickle, roll, and swing her.

* Create lighting on any wall of your home to allow shadow play: Make hand-shadow animals, cut out letters, and cast the shadow on the wall for an education session; also try shadow stick puppets or play shadow tag.

* Art time: For this age the following art materials are appropriate: water colors (on paper or you can have her paint shells, rocks, clay sculptures,) crayons, stamps with inkpads, chalk, modeling clay, or play dough. All of these respond well to clean up and are easy enough for an older baby or young toddler.

* School time: Teach colors, shapes, numbers, letters, and matching. Focus on teaching your child simple sentences and begin to teach "feelings" language, such as sad, happy, and mad.

* Any play ideas from the previous section that your child may still enjoy.

Toys

Matching cards, dress-up things, big wooden beads for stringing, and plastic animals. This age group likes to engage in imaginative play where they are the main character, so this is a good time to buy tool sets, kitchens, musical instruments, cleaning supplies, and play electronics (phones, computers.) Consider creating a dress-up box or dress-up kits (doctor, waiter or waitress, cashier, chef, gardener) to expand your child's imaginative play.

Your 18–30 Month Old

There will be two notable changes in your little one's play style as he nears the 18-month mark. First, he'll be ready to do crafts with you. Children love crafts and you will find they bring a special element to your days and time together. Secondly, he'll become more independent in his playing. His imagination will have expanded and where previously he was role-playing by mimicking adults, he is now creating entire stories with toy characters, stuffed animals, play foods, and cars, where anything can become something else.

Play ideas for this age group

* Buy a wash bin/wash basin. Fill it with soapy water and a washcloth. Teach your child how to wash dishes (use plastic dishes) or take this opportunity to wash some well-loved toys.
* Do more advanced building with blocks: Make tunnels, bridges, and castles with your child.
* Have dress-up time where you both get dressed up together and role-play.
* Photo exploration: Buy a toddler camera (or use your own) and allow your child to take pictures that correspond to a given theme. Afterwards you can upload them to your computer or a disc to be printed and make a photo-exploration collage.
* Fill a large bowl with your child's collection of balls and play basketball using the bowl as the "hoop."
* Play toddler golf.
* Cook together. There are all sorts of small things that your child can assist you with while you cook. He will benefit by being a helper because he will feel proud of the new things he is learning and

accomplishing. You will feel empowered by getting work done while spending quality time with your child.

* Allow your child to take responsibility for a small garden. This can be a few pots on your porch or a small three feet by three feet plot in your yard. Teach him about soil, seeds, watering, transplanting, and weeds.
* Make or buy a felt board; tell felt-board stories, make felt school lessons, or sit back and watch as your child creates his own stories out of the felt pieces.
* Outdoor educational lessons: I recommend a book called *Gardening with Children* by Monika Hanneman.
* Play hide-and-seek.
* Make or buy a toy mailbox and play letter writing, delivery, and receiving.
* Patio chalk fun: Turn your patio into a chalkboard—if you don't have a patio, consider laying some pavers for this purpose. You can draw large animals, teach school lessons, and make a chalk road for your child's cars.
* Teach your little one how to wrap presents. He will delight in giving grandma a wrapped-up potato pet that he made during craft hour with you.
* It's time your little one started to socialize. Consider joining or hosting play dates two to three times a week.
* If your child has a play kitchen you can play bakery, restaurant, or grocery with the food items that are there. Pretend to be your child's most loyal customer while asking him for a plate of food. For grocery shopping, give him a basket with a list of foods that you know are in his kitchen

animal, and letter of the day. Have the puppet hold each of these up while asking your child engaging questions. Also discuss the day of the week and the weather. I like to pretend that one animal puppet is giving the "letter of the day" to the other puppet. The puppet then asks questions such as, "What begins with the letter R?" or, "What do we know that is green?" When timely, sing the alphabet song or other fun songs.

* Art hour: Accessorize your child's art box. He's still too young for advanced arts but to keep things new you can add more items, such as clay tools, play-dough accessories, and new stamps. Experiment with different types of painting and introduce coloring books.

* School time: Teach the names of different coins and continents. You could introduce counting, letters, basic phonics, and drawing lines and shapes

* Crafts hour: Your child is ready for craft time. He has most likely outgrown the sensory table. This will make a great craft table (assuming it has a top.) Also, many of your sensory supplies can be used for gluing fun and make perfect craft supplies. The next section offers general guidelines on introducing crafts and includes a selection of surprisingly easy craft ideas.

* Any activities or play ideas from the previous list that your child may still enjoy.

Toys

Piggy bank, flashlight, educational toys, sit and bounce ball, floor puzzles, science kit, pattern block board, binoculars, kid's bingo, giant soft blocks, toddler camera, toddler board games, sorting suitcase, layered puzzles, dollhouse, play zoo, castle, felt board, and other toys that can act as key components to your toddler's story creations.

(use pictures of foods for the list) and have him find the items; you can be the cashier. If you play bakery, make sure to end with a tea party with everything that your child has served you.

* Set up a treasure hunt: Hide a treasure box somewhere in your home, maybe under one of her favorite toys. Hand draw three puzzle pieces for clues and hide these in three separate locations. Next make a map that your child can follow to show where the clues are hidden. When your child finds the clues and puts them together, the hiding place of the treasure box is revealed. In this case, she'll find that her treasure box was hiding under her teddy bear all the time.

* Have a puppet show: If you're creative with dialogue and storytelling, a puppet show should be easy. If not, you could do an educational puppet show. Whether you use puzzle pieces, blocks, laminated cutouts, or magnets you will need the following: a number, color, shape,

Introducing Crafts to a Toddler

If your baby has started to walk, you may start to notice that toys don't hold her interest as much as they used to. Many children will seek out real adventures once they are fully mobile. Introducing a daily craft time into your day is one way to reduce those inevitable "bored-with-toys" days.

When Keli was 18 months old I started looking for craft supplies that she might be able to manipulate on her own. She still put things in her mouth, so I aimed to buy non-toxic supplies. I was wary of all that could go wrong: eating or getting glue on the couch, the "I can't do it" meltdowns, or the end product being unrecognizable. Most of the crafts I had seen kids doing involved glitter, scissors, and drawing. Keli wasn't ready for those projects and so when I introduced crafts, I knew it would be a full-on experiment. Having test-driven early crafting, I have come up with some useful tips to pass on.

When you first introduce crafts, there won't be many actual craft skills that your toddler can manage. She'll use the glue stick and paste things together; she might color pictures in. You'll do the cutting and if you want the craft to look anything like it should, you'll have to guide her in the placement of things. It's a good idea to plan for super simple crafts and be prepared to do most of the work. Your child will enjoy helping in small ways and watching something unfold in front of her.

Surprisingly easy crafts

* Felt fun: Make felt pieces for your felt board.
* Glue puzzle: Instead of cutting out an animal for your child to decorate, try cutting out different animal parts and have your child work out how to glue the animal together.
* Tissue paper flowers: If you use a washable marker to color on a tissue paper or coffee filter and then spray it with water, it has a tie-dyeing effect. Ruffle it up and attach it to a pipe cleaner to make a flower.
* Ladybugs: Dip your child's thumb into red ink and make ladybugs out of her thumbprints.
* Decorate a pencil: Make a bouquet of artificial flowers and feathers and tie it to the pencil with a rubber band or pipe cleaner.
* Daily weather art: Have a week of weather crafts where your child makes a picture of a sunny, rainy, or cloudy day. Our favorite was the morning of a storm where we cut out clouds, covered them in glue and cotton, and then pasted them to a piece of grey paper. Then we cut out tin foil zigzags for lightning.
* Three-in-one clay pendants: You can make these clay pendants by cutting small circles out of clay and decorating them with pretty stamp shapes. Once dry, your little one can paint them and later string them onto thread with beads, making a necklace.
* Make a puppet: Use a sock, paper bag, or wooden spoon.
* Tissue-paper butterfly: Draw a large butterfly on a piece of paper and outline areas to help your child know where to paste the decorations. Cut square shapes from several different colors of

tissue paper (gift-bag paper) and have your child use a glue stick to stick them on.

* Maracas: Fill one cup with beads, beans, and jingle bells and tape it to a second cup so that the lip of each cup is connected to the other. Paint the outside of them and shake to make colorful music.

* Paper-plate mask: Draw or print off and then color a funny face. Glue it onto a paper plate. Next, cut out holes for the eyes and glue the mask to a large Popsicle stick to make a handle.

* Make magnets: Glue small pictures (chosen by your child) to the flat side of a clear gemstone (found at the bottom of fish tanks.) Cut a small piece of magnetic strip into a square and glue it to the back of the gemstone.

* Pinecone owl: Glue plastic eyes and a small orange triangle made out of construction paper (owl's nose) onto the pinecone to make the face. Glue feathers into the cone's crevices or paint the pinecone for extra decoration.

* Toilet-paper-roll butterfly: Use a toilet-paper roll for the butterfly's body. Attach two small pieces of pipe cleaner at one end to make antennas. Cut wings out of construction paper, and glue them to the outer edge of the toilet roll. Decorate the butterfly with paint, markers, stickers, glitter, or gemstones.

* Mixed media collage: Draw or cut out a school bus and then, after having searched through magazines, cut out pictures of children. Paste their faces on the windows of the school bus to create a fun picture. Print off a large sheep's face and then add cotton balls around his face to create fur. Finding a way to incorporate pre-existing images into your craft hour can increase the possibilities and add a fun new twist to craft time.

✳ HELPFUL HINTS

1 Take out supplies ahead of time. Don't bring all of your supplies to craft time. Bring only the supplies you'll need for the planned craft. If you leave it all out, your toddler will be on her way to her own craft and could be frustrated by a lack of guidance.

2 Do any cutting for the craft ahead of time. This way you don't have to worry about your child getting hold of the scissors and she won't have to wait while you cut things out. Children have very little patience, so a craft time that keeps them waiting is not a good one.

3 When possible, use glue sticks. This age group does a great job with them.

4 If glue sticks aren't possible, assist your child with regular craft glue. Rather than letting your child put the glue on the paper, ask her where the glue spot should go. If you are attached to where the glue should go, put it there but let her do the attaching. Another technique is to fill a small paper cup with glue and provide a Popsicle stick for applying it.

5 Set up a free-glue project. Give your child a piece of construction paper, a glue stick, and cutout shapes. She will have fun gluing these all over the paper. Alternatively, give her beans, pasta, sequins, feathers, and small rocks for gluing.

6 Craft happens at the craft table. If you pick a table to sit at and bring a damp towel to it (in case of glue/paint disasters,) then you can keep messes contained. Your little one will love the idea of a craft table and probably will be having too much fun to want to roam anyway, but if you have a particularly antsy child then you'll have to teach her that craft time is over when she leaves the table.

7 Paint and glue are yucky. I was surprised that Keli never tried to eat glue, paint, or play dough. Chances are high that you are more worried about this than necessary, but even if your child is doing this, simply take it away and tell her that "glue is for gluing," "paint is for painting." At first, some kids don't know or they might forget. If this doesn't work or causes a fit, craft time ends. Don't give up on crafts, though; soon the rules will stick.

8 Plan how your child will help. Make sure that your child can do some steps on her own. Use white construction paper in many of your crafts so that your little one can do some coloring on it. Other things she can do are gluing, sprinkling glitter, wrapping pipe cleaners, painting, adding stickers, and stamping.

9 Don't be attached to the outcome. Don't argue with your child about where this or that goes. As your child may want to play with the end result, you'll want to try to make something that resembles what you had in mind but not at the cost of making craft time unpleasant. If your little one ends up making a glue fest of sparklies, beans, and pom-poms, it's really not a big deal. Similarly, if she doesn't want to take part, feel free to finish the project yourself. Avoid putting pressure on your toddler at craft time.

10 Have a glue-drying spot. At first your toddler might complain that she can't play with the finished craft. You have to explain that the glue needs to dry. Choose and then establish a glue-drying place. The drying spot should be accessible to your child so that she can put the craft to dry and won't feel as though you are taking it away. Also, she'll be able to check on it as much as she wants. Keli was known to pull a stool up to her glue-drying place and watch and wait.

Educating Your Child

Young children love to learn. What to teach and when to teach it will come to you intuitively and will differ from child to child. The most important thing to consider is working from a bottom-up approach. The chart below presents education goals for three main areas of your child's education: speech, pre-school, and life skills. It's important to teach all three types of education simultaneously while also being mindful only to teach higher levels once the basic levels have been achieved.

Be mindful not to limit your child's education. For example, regarding speech, focus on the most important words first: mommy, daddy, diaper, eat, shoes, outside, milk, play (words that aid efficient communication.) When you see that your child knows his farm animals, go into the jungle; when he knows his jungle animals, go into the sea. Whenever possible, take your child to a zoo or a farm and generally try to make the abstract more concrete while you're teaching. If you're teaching mostly with books, it's important for your child to see how this knowledge extends into the real world.

The chart below is a general outline for the education process we used with our daughter; this was very much guided by her response and progress in each area. I share this simply to give you an idea of age-appropriate focuses and your child's potential rather than suggesting that your education goals be based on it. Although your child's motor development is another important area, this is not included in the chart. Motor skills are generally not taught; rather, they naturally occur with parental

Speech

Naming animals
Making animal sounds
Naming and responding to requests for household objects
Can put 2–3 words together for a sentence
Understands and can verbalize emotion
Communicates more clearly, sentences with up to 4 words
Constructs complete 5–6 word sentences
Advancing vocabulary, has sense of changing word endings

encouragement. They can be developed by giving your child a rattle, shape-fitting ball, and holding something just out of reach so that he can grab it. It is wise to encourage sitting up, crawling, and standing practice.

The education goals listed in the chart are targeted for educational experiences led by you, and it is around the ten-month mark that this type of education can occur. Before the age of ten months, the language center of your child's brain is developing every day, neurons are wiring together, and connections are being made in the brain that will be with your child for the rest of his life. It is important to interact with your child as much as possible: make eye contact, move your mouth to exaggerate sounds, and speak clearly.

From around 24 months on, Keli learned how to get dressed, and began basic phonics and counting games. We also began a daily school hour when she practiced all of the things she had learned up to that point. This is an excellent opportunity to talk about weather, days of the week, holidays, and months. I began with practical life-skill lessons (see pages 134–135.) Whereas some life skills will begin sooner, children really begin responding to the benefits of practical life-skill lessons once they have reached the two-year mark.

Pre-school	Life skills	Keli's age*
Learning colors	Sippy Cup	10 months
Learning shapes	Carries plate	12 months
Organizing and sorting	Can pour	14 months
Learning letters	Can clean a mess	16 months
Learning numbers	Can help in getting dressed	18 months
Learning names of different coins	Can help with some cooking	20 months
Learning continents	Begins to learn manners	22 months
Begins basic phonic lessons	Opening, closing, fastening, tying	24 months and beyond

* when we introduced it

Academic Education

Academic education happens when your little one begins to learn information that will prepare her for pre-school and the years beyond. Although it's not necessary to start this process when your child is a baby, it's rewarding to do so. She will enjoy the challenge of naming, organizing, and utilizing new information. Young babies tend to be immersed fully in learning about their world, even more so than your curious toddler. You can get a great head start by starting as early as ten months with introducing colors and shapes.

There are many interesting ways to teach pre-school skills. I found that by keeping a bin full of school supplies, I was inspired to have a daily school hour. I recommend stocking up on the following: weather dial, white board with dry erase markers, calendar, pointer, sorting materials, beans, blocks, vessels, wooden letters, matching number cards, educational puzzles, and stickers for rewards. If at first you don't have many teaching techniques in mind, use the education sections of this book to get you started, ask other mothers what they do, and scour pre-school websites for fun and educational activities. One wonderful idea and experience will lead to the next.

✳ HELPFUL HINTS

1 Number, shape, and color puzzles.

2 Matching games.

3 Felt board, chalk board, and white boards are good for teaching.

4 Flash cards and educational picture books are great for teaching numbers, letters, colors, and object names.

5 Use an ice tray or muffin tin as a sorting tray. You'll place one color of a specific item (button, block, pom-pom) into an empty spot. Your child will follow your lead by filling each spot with items that match in color. She can also sort by texture or shape.

6 Paint toilet-paper rolls in different colors and draw a different shape or write a number on each one. Make corresponding cut outs. Tape the toilet-paper rolls to a piece of cardboard that can then be attached to a wall. Have your child drop the cut outs into the matching rolls (you can also do this with small paper lunch bags.)

7 Using a white board and dry erase markers, practice drawing lines and circles together.

8 **Make shape magnets** (four of each shape) and have your child make rows or groups of each shape on your refrigerator.

9 **Create small-to-big activities** using beads, blocks, or stacking cups.

10 **Place five bowls together** and tape a number inside each one (1–5.) Have your child fill each bowl with the corresponding number of jellybeans.

11 **Draw a word on a piece of paper** and have your little one put the object on that word (ball, spoon, cup, shoe.) If this is too difficult, you can use colors for a more cued activity. Write the word "purple" in purple crayon on paper; have your child gather purple objects to place on the paper. This also works with reading numbers; write the number 3 or the word "three" on a piece of construction paper. The goal is for your child to put three blocks down on that piece of paper.

12 **Make five horizontal rows on a sheet of paper.** The top row will have the number one on it followed by one large dot. The row below this will have the number two followed by two dots, and so on until you get to the fifth row, which will be the number five with five dots. Have your child place a small block or coin on each dot. This will give her a visual for the small to larger concept of numbers. As she gets better at this, remove the dots and have her do it with the number symbol alone.

13 **Have a letter of the day and do activities that all represent your chosen letter.** For instance, if your letter for the day is "C" you might draw a cat together, or make a cat craft. Next, have your child trace both upper and lower case "C." Finally, do a puzzle of an animal that begins with "C" and eat carrots or cookies.

14 **Draw a large thick letter that is big enough to be filled with small square blocks.** Your child can place blocks to cover the letter you drew, making that letter out of blocks. You can draw squares where each block needs to go if your toddler needs the extra guidance. You can also take this idea and replace the blocks with dot markers. This will mimic drawing and give your child a feel for letter shapes.

15 **Put on a puppet show** that involves a color, shape, number, and letter of the day (see page 125.)

Practical Life Skills

Your toddler will gain more control over his environment once he begins learning new life skills. This will help ease the terrible-twos frustrations that are largely caused by feelings of helplessness. Your child will delight in his successes and you'll find great joy in his developing independence.

Because most of these lessons will require movement and allow for messiness, life skills are as fun as they are practical. If you conduct a school hour each day, allocate some portion of this hour for life-skill lessons; these types of activities are an enjoyable way to add diversity to your child's educational experience.

✳ HELPFUL HINTS

1 **Teach your little one how to wash washcloths** by hand and hang them on a line. Once they are dry you can use them for ironing and folding lessons.

2 **Practice tying shoes,** using zippers, buttons, and Velcro.

3 **Encourage your child to get dressed,** put on shoes, and brush his teeth independently.

4 **Introduce pouring activities** using beans, rice, scoops, and empty containers. Once he becomes a steady pourer, try using a jug of water or juice and have him practice pouring into a cup.

5 **Teach vegetable cutting** by using wooden vegetables that have Velcro connecting the pieces together. These kits come with a wooden knife that "cuts" between the Velcro so that the vegetable will fall to pieces. You can also teach cutting with soft foods like tofu and mushrooms using a butter knife.

6 **Spend time cleaning your child's bedroom together:** You can also teach window washing, cleaning off art surfaces, and sorting laundry. Buy a children's cleaning kit (broom, duster, washcloths) or teach your little guy how to use yours.

7 **Set up a bin of soapy water** with a washcloth and some of your child's play dishes or other unbreakable dishes. Have him practice washing dishes with you.

8 **Gather several containers** that have different opening and closing techniques. Teach your child to screw on a lid, use a key, work a latch, or slide a lock.

9 **Use realistic play tools** to teach your child to use a hammer, wrench, and screwdriver. You can use real tools in some cases (for example, sanding and measuring.)

10 **Teach your child how to water plants** using a lightweight kid-sized watering can.

11 **Demonstrate good hand washing:** Teach the importance of using soap and show him how to wash and rinse his hands thoroughly. I recommend getting a children's bathroom stool.

12 **Have him practice setting a table with you**.

13 **Teach manners:** There are some great manners books out there but you could also do some role playing.

14 **Practice hanging clothes** on a hanger or putting them in the correct drawers.

15 **Encourage your child to clean up** his spills with a sponge, or to wipe down the table himself after a messy mealtime.

Nature Education

In the spirit of great educational movements like Waldorf and Montessori, I've included this section on educating your child about the natural world. My experience is that nature education provides the following benefits:

* Entertainment away from television, video games, and computers.
* Fresh air, sun, and exercise that is necessary for good health.
* An opportunity for different types of imaginative play.
* Fine motor skill development (pouring sand or water, watering plants, picking weeds, drawing in the dirt).
* Knowledge about weather, what to wear outdoors, time, and seasons.
* Connection and respect for the natural world (development of empathy with other living creatures and respect for natural habitats).
* Understanding of one's place in and relationship with the world around you.

1 **Nature rubs.** This is a great way for children to learn about nature's beautiful patterns—you can use leaves, fossils, and shells to make these. Put a nature item under a piece of paper and have your child color on top of the paper with a crayon until the pattern shows through. You can also buy pre-made rubbing plates.

2 **Natural instruments.** Collect natural materials and make them into instruments. You might make shakers out of pebbles and clamshells, a xylophone with sticks, or fill a poster tube with seeds to make a rain stick. Make music together.

3 **Simple planting activity.** You can use yogurt containers for the pot and seeds saved from any vegetable or fruit. You won't even need to buy soil as I'm sure your little one would love to dig some dirt up from your yard. Be sure to teach her how to remove weeds, rocks, and sticks.

4 **Nature hunt.** Take a walk outside to collect sticks, leaves, nuts, shells, pinecones, rocks, and flowers. Be sure to bring a bowl or basket. Go home and talk about your discoveries, discuss how they feel and smell, and label or draw them. Consider a craft project using the nature materials. You can make a butterfly out of leaves and sticks or a fall leaf collage.

5 **Nature smells.** Fill a basket with blooms, pine needles, pinecones, grass, and bark. Blindfold your toddler, take out one of these, and see if she can guess what's in your hand.

6 **Animal calls.** Go for a walk somewhere where you know there will be animal sounds, talk about and identify them.

7 **Nature scavenger hunt.** Take an egg carton and a list of twelve nature items to collect with a theme such as soft, spiky, blue, strong, beautiful, old, fragile, yummy, sharp, smooth, closed, open, wet, dry, and so on.

8 **Felt-board weather lesson.** Make or buy felt pieces that can be used to teach weather lessons. Show what a rainy day looks like by adding rain clouds, umbrellas, rain boots, and puddles to your felt board. You can make a felt person and ask your child to dress him for a rainy day and contrast this with what a winter outfit would look like.

9 **Felt-board seasons lesson.** Similar to above, make or buy felt pieces but focus on budding flowers, falling leaves, snowy ground, and beach fun.

10 **Replicate an animal habitat together.** Choose an animal and discuss its habitat. Once you and your child know about its habitat, go outside and begin gathering the necessary materials to make your best replica. Place your findings in an old shoebox or fish tank. You might allow her to spend a few hours trying to catch a turtle, frog, or minnow.

CHAPTER 7:

Being a Stay-at-Home Parent

A Day in the Life of a Stay-at-Home Parent

This chapter is dedicated to those of you who have been asked, "What do you do all day as a stay-at-home parent?" You may wonder which role they are referring to: parent, teacher, negotiator, maid, nurse, entertainer, chef...? Being a stay-at-home parent is a multi-faceted position and, what's more, you have to change your role at the drop of a hat. One moment you will be entertaining your child, the next he is crying and you are soothing him. Moments later your child needs something to eat and soon you are negotiating about a dirty diaper.

All jobs require dedication and commitment. However, parenting is the only job on the planet that requires having to be completely absorbed with another human being during all waking hours. To top it off, no matter how flexible parents are, we still receive many not-so-subtle objections that let us know our little client is not pleased. Being a parent is life changing; being a stay-at-home parent is life consuming; and being an Attachment stay-at-home Parent tops all the others.

Despite knowing that we haven't taken a breath that wasn't for our child's benefit in the past thirteen hours, as a parent we don't always know how to answer the dreaded "what do you do all day" question. Sometimes, although we are occupied, we are bored, an interesting phenomenon that only parents experience. Most bored people can browse the Internet, watch a movie, or read a book. A stay-at-home parent can't do these things because we must keep engaging with and supervising our child.

The problem with this is that we often become disengaged while doing this. The result is an experience that is unfulfilling for both our children and ourselves.

Create a daily schedule

To help with this I've come up with a schedule with several benefits: you will be able to answer the dreaded question and your day will be more organized; you will still wear many hats in a day, but you'll know what's coming next and feel more engaged because you are sticking to a plan. You won't run into those stressful moments you experience when your child is bored and he'll be happier changing activities throughout the day and having a schedule that mom and dad take a special part in.

The key to this schedule is using the phrase: "It's _____ time." You can use anything to fill in that blank. What's important here is that your child knows that a transition is happening, you are in charge of it, and it will be fun. Don't ask him what he wants to do; just let him know what's happening in an excited way that calls him to hop on board. It works every time.

Opposite is the schedule we use at home with our daughter.

7–8 a.m.
Free Play (parent has some time to relax but then gets child dressed and works on breakfast)

8–8.30 a.m.
Breakfast (whatever your child's eating routine is)

8.30–9.30 a.m.
School hour

9.30–11 a.m.
Outdoor play or an outing

11–11.30 a.m.
Free play (parent makes lunch)

11.30 a.m.–12.15 p.m.
Lunchtime (make this a one-on-one connecting time)

12.15–2 p.m.
Nap time (great time for parent to take a break and clean up)

2–3 p.m.
Craft or art hour

3–3.30 p.m.
Snack time

3.30–5 p.m.
Outdoor play or an outing

5–5.30 p.m.
Free play (parent makes dinner)

5.30–6.30 p.m.
Dinner time

6.30–7.30 p.m.
Bedtime routine (bath, teeth, jammies, books)

7.30 p.m.
Bedtime

Notice there are only two hours of free play in this schedule and these times are mostly used for the parent to do whatever else needs to be done. Your child will be more willing to give you space for household work when you have spent most of the day connecting with him.

This is a basic schedule, one that we've used many times. There will be days when you don't feel like going on two outings. Maybe you're sick, maybe it's raining, or maybe your little one is fussy. There will also be days when you want to skip school time or craft hour. If that's the case, use those time slots for some unique play times such as circle time with books, play date with friends, life-skills practices, puppet show, bubbles and dance party, or yoga hour. The important things are to think of your day as chunks of time and making sure that your child has a diverse day.

Organizing a Playroom

I'm a mom that is obsessed with organizing her daughter's life. This chapter, as my husband so kindly suggested, could have been called OCD momma. I even organize her play. Organized play? Isn't that an oxymoron? I suppose it would be if Keli was doing the organizing and the playing, but she isn't. I organize, she plays, and it works out wonderfully.

There are hundreds of articles and photographs out there about setting up a nursery and just as many conversations between mothers about their children's playrooms. This is a popular topic because having a great playroom can be a huge factor in your staying sane as a parent. Creating a great one isn't about having the most expensive wall decals or hand-carved building blocks. A fantastic playroom welcomes play; it makes toys accessible, is interesting, and keeps your little girl occupied. Such a playroom will have your child playing busily while you finally take a break.

All playrooms were not created equal. You might visit a friend's house and find their child has better toys than yours, the play areas are divided better, their craft table is something you now realize your child can't live without. You haven't seen your child play so independently in the two years that she's been alive. Naturally, you start making a mental checklist of things you're going to tell your partner about. You're near certain that he'll agree that these must be miracle toys and tell you to go ahead and make the purchase that you've already committed to in your mind. Although learning about and purchasing wonderful toys and room accessories can contribute to the perfect playroom, the real key is in how you organize the room.

1 **Pick a location.** The most obvious option might be to turn your child's bedroom into her playroom, but I recommend setting up her play area elsewhere. Sleep experts recommend no toys in the bedroom. I've always chosen rooms or areas of my home that were visible from the most-used rooms (the kitchen and living room.) Natural sunlight is the best. When we moved into our new place I made the mistake of choosing a dimly lit play area for our daughter. It was the perfect place otherwise, but I started to notice her migrating towards the best-lit room in the house. If natural light is not an option, consider installing high-quality lighting.

2 **Move things around** regularly. Regardless of how gorgeous your playroom is, don't be attached to how you have it set up. If there's one thing all stay-at-home parents know, it's that kids get bored with their toys. To encourage your child to keep playing in it, rearrange the playroom at least monthly. If you have more than one play area in the house, you might want to swap some of the toys.

3 **Organize the toys.** What you have in the playroom is not the main priority. The important thing is that your child can access the majority of it, most of the time. I'm a huge advocate of toy organizers. My favorite is a shelving unit with bins that slot into it. These organizers hold an incredible amount of toys and allow your child to see and have access to her toys at all times. We organize the toys by bin: balls, blocks, dress-up kits, kitchen, cars and tracks, animals, nature things, puppets, dollhouse accessories, and felts each have their own bin. When one bin's contents have been outgrown, find a new age-appropriate set of toys or activity pieces to fill it. The opposite approach to storing toys is a toy box, where everything is simply thrown randomly into one place.

4 **Set up constant play stations.** A good toy system goes hand in hand with play stations—areas of the room that have been designated for certain types of play. Play stations are usually large and see a lot of use. The area could be set up with a play kitchen, art easel, dollhouse, sensory table, felt board, or sandbox. A good playroom has several play stations. The more there are in one room, the more interesting that room will be for your child: it's no longer just a room with toys but has activities set up in it at all times. Think about a daycare room and how it has separate areas for book time, snack time, art, and sensory time. These rooms are designed to keep play organized, fluid, and purposeful for the child.

5 **Play set-ups.** Play set-ups are areas of play that you'll set up throughout the day in order to invite your child to play. There are two types of play set-up. The first is where you set out the materials for a certain activity: a craft, life skills, or sensory project. The main idea here is that you set up while your child is sleeping or out with your partner and that when she comes back she will be surprised with the fun activities that await her. To create the second type, go through your child's toys and pull out those that haven't been used for a while, then get creative. How can you make this toy more interesting? The idea here is to lay the toys out nicely or add something new to the mix to draw her toward otherwise ignored toys. By taking out your little one's play foods and setting up a restaurant table for her, or building a track out of blocks to go with her favorite car toy, you're making old toys more appealing.

6 **Keep some play accessories hidden.** Keep a few things tucked away in the play area. A tent, a collapsible tube for climbing through, busy boxes (see page 122,) and a picnic blanket are a few items that we like to set up occasionally. This way I always have something on hand that she hasn't gotten bored with. It's also practical because most of these things are rather large and the room is neater with them tidied away most of the time.

7 **Keep the room neat.** You may think it is impossible to keep a clean play area or simply pointless. If your toy room is organized, it's quite easy to put away toys. This will benefit your child because she can focus on what she's playing with rather than moving around in a room that's covered in toys. We've experimented with both messy and neat. I learned that when Keli plays in a neat room she does less aimless wandering and is more engaged in her playing. One way to keep the play area tidy is by teaching your child that before starting a new activity she must first put away the last one.

9 **Keep art supplies handy.** These are fantastic for entertaining your little one, but keep them out of her reach. Some people use art supplies as part of their child's free play experience. Yet again, I recommend the benefits of novelty. If your little one always has access to her markers, crayons, and play dough, then most likely these things will end up on the floor in minutes. By saving them for art times or only taking them out when she asks for them, your child will continue to appreciate them.

8 **Baby-proof the room.** Your playroom should be baby proofed. What fun is there in setting up in an area that keeps you worried and watchful? Your child should have free rein of this room and you should feel okay about leaving her in there for a brief time, if the phone rings for example. For me this means no exposed outlets, no glass, no hanging cords from blinds, and no hard furniture when little one is unsteady on her feet (especially if the furniture has corners.)

10 **Have a multi-purpose table.** The list of items that you can buy for your child's playroom is endless, and the one that I would single out for its ability to change the feel of the room instantly is a child's table. A child's play zone needs a table where she can sit for art, crafts, coloring books, setting up a tea party, or eating a snack. Of course a young baby will not be able to use this, but as your child gets older, having her own table is a rite of passage.

Cooking with a Toddler

It can be hard to get everything done in a day while taking care of your child. Whenever you can, involve your child in your household work. I especially like having my daughter join me in the kitchen because it keeps us both from starving.

There are two great reasons to cook with your toddler. 1. You have to cook anyway; trying to cook without him will be more difficult than including him, and 2. He will love you forever and ever if you let him help you in the kitchen. Kids love to help their parents cook. They love to do anything that makes them feel included in big-people stuff. Understandably, many parents are wary of engaging their child in the kitchen. It can be a little scary at first. Won't he make a huge mess? Can he really help me? Won't he end up being in the way? Is it safe? I asked all of these questions but have since discovered a few tricks that helped to build my confidence.

More often than not, your toddler will make a mess while helping you in the kitchen. I'm a neat freak, so if I'm saying this activity doesn't have to be messy, it really doesn't. How you'll go about managing messes will depend on what you're cooking. Baking projects will be the messiest.

Baking

If you're baking, I recommend pulling out all of the ingredients you'll need (as well as measuring cups.) Sit down right beside your toddler. You should be the one to measure out the ingredients and your child can dump the ingredients into the mixing bowl. Once all of the dry ingredients are added, mix them well. Only after you've mixed them should your child get a turn at mixing; this ensures that no more of one ingredient than another is accidentally spilled from

the bowl. As your child is mixing, you can quickly put away everything that you have finished using.

Next, make your wet mixture as your little one is still mixing dry ingredients. He can pour the wet ingredients into the bowl but you'll have to mix it first because he's guaranteed to splash it everywhere. He'll probably splash it everywhere either way, but if you've mixed it first there's a better chance that he

won't. Let your little one take over the final mixing while you grease the pan and clean up the remaining mess. Your little one will sit happily trying to steal bites of batter while pretending to mix. Pour the batter together, spend a minute sweeping up any spilled flour and sugar, and voilà—you just made muffins for next week's breakfasts and entertained your toddler at the same time.

Making a meal

If you're making a savory meal that will require prepping vegetables, set up two cutting boards: one for you and one for your child. Give your child a play knife and either play at cutting vegetables or a soft food such as tofu or kiwi. While you are both busy at your cutting stations, keep your little one engaged by talking about the process: "We're making dinner for daddy because when he comes home he'll be hungry." Talking about the importance of cooking and how helpful your child is being will give him that extra touch of purpose and make him feel responsible.

If the vegetables are ready to go but you need a minute to put some water on to boil for your grains, ask your child to put the vegetables in a pan. Alternatively, you can let a pot sit as it fills with water and you can measure the grains together.

If you're making dips or other blended foods, let your child put the ingredients in the blender; unplug the blender before you do this.

Keep your toddler busy

Another trick to keep in mind is that if there's nothing your toddler can do for a particular meal (see below,) have him do something arbitrary—just because you won't need strawberries in your eggplant Parmesan doesn't mean your little one can't cut them up for tomorrow's breakfast.

Things your toddler can do in the kitchen

* Mixing
* Cutting soft foods with a play knife (mushrooms, strawberries, kiwi, papaya, tofu.)
* De-stemming spinach, parsley, cilantro.
* Adding spices: let him add the ones that are hard to overdo, just in case he overdoes it. Spices such as nutritional yeast, paprika, or dried parsley are all pretty safe to let children add to a meal, as opposed to cayenne pepper.
* Salting
* Spreading sauce over pizza crusts.
* Topping pizza crusts with cheese.
* Moving cut vegetables to a colander or bowl.
* Pouring ingredients
* Measuring pasta or rice.

Lastly, the best advice I can give you is to plan for something simple when your little one is helping you cook. It's easy to keep a toddler happy in the kitchen for twenty minutes. The last ten minutes might be a little hectic as you finish up tasks that you have to do without him, but those minutes will pass quickly and you'll end up smiling with the realization that you pulled it all off. A proud toddler and a yummy dinner will greet whoever is coming home, mom or dad.

Play-Date Ideas

Play dates are a great way to get your toddler playing with other children her age. You can hold play dates at home, a friend's house, a local kid's spot, or a nature park. The key is to have a fun plan, invite at least one friend and child, and commit to making the date happen.

Play dates are a win-win for everyone. Even though you'll always be her favorite playmate, she'll most likely enjoy being with another child and the change of pace that comes with this. I cannot stress enough how important it is for your child to have new experiences. It will make her happy and build character. If you're a stay-at-home parent, this will give you an opportunity to chat with another parent and enjoy a change of scenery.

Ideas for play dates

* Hold a kid's toy swap. Invite friends and their children over to your house for milk and cookies. Everyone has to bring at least three unloved toys. Make a big pile of unwanted toys in the middle of the room and select those that you want.
* Clothes swap: This is the same idea as above, but you swap your child's outgrown clothes.
* Craft date: Hold an hour of craft fun at your house.
* Go to the zoo.
* Go to a museum.
* Invite a friend and child to lunch. Choose a family friendly café.
* Go to the library for story time.
* Visit a local nature park.
* Grab a gelato.
* Have a scrapbooking party at your house.

* Get hot chocolates and walk to a nearby playground.
* Visit the mall's indoor playground.
* Have a mini pool party with snacks and lemonade.
* Have a picnic at the park.
* Play-dough date: Make homemade play dough, take out all of your play-dough accessories (cookie cutters, cookie sheets, play-dough tools) and let the fun begin.
* Have a cookie date: Make real cookies.
* Get a group of children together at a park (have their parents pack an instrument). Create a marching band that marches through the park.
* Hold a treasure hunt in a nature park.
* Have a holiday craft party: Make Christmas cards or Halloween costumes.
* Splash date: Bring water balloons and water hoses out in someone's backyard for a splash-park experience or, better yet, visit a splash park.
* Go on a field trip to a nearby beach.
* Visit an arcade.
* Hold a book reading at your house that ends with a craft that touches on the theme of the book.
* Attend a local event that has already been planned.
* Visit any public, local play area.

I began printing off a blank calendar at the beginning of each month. This is a handy way of keeping a list of local kid's activities and events that are going on in your town or city. If it's looking rather empty, fill it in with some of the above ideas. People that you know will be grateful to you for inviting them along.

Stay-at-Home Pre-School

Is your toddler bored or stuck inside too much? Are you sensing that he would benefit from playing with children his own age on a regular basis? Is pre-school unappealing because you want your child to be with you? Would you like your little one to be social, engage in structured activities, and learn to trust other adults? If you answered yes, a stay-at-home pre-school co-op might be the answer.

As my daughter approached her third birthday, I knew that I wanted her to have a pre-school experience. However, I didn't want to send her off to a pre-school. Essentially, this was a dilemma.

In figuring out what to do about the situation, I had to ask myself what conditions I had for Keli's schooling. I came up with the following: affordable, I can be present, includes other children, small number of other trusted adults involved, and occurs at least three times a week. The most likely model of education that took into account all of these conditions was a school co-op model.

Co-op is short for cooperative. There are several different definitions, ranging from five-days-a-week schools taught by a different parent each day to something as simple as a group of home-schooling

Models to choose from

Group classes, three days a week

I'm looking for four parents to come together three days a week between 8 a.m. and 12 p.m. to create a home-school experience that is social, diversified, and community based for our pre-school-aged child. Qualified candidates must have at least one but no more than two pre-school-aged children who would attend all classes. Each parent is to lead one full pre-school day while the other parents assist. Benefits include free education, children socializing with other children and adults, and receiving a diverse educational experience. Also you will be with your child.

Group classes, five days a week with one teacher per day

I'm looking for four teachers to teach one full (8 a.m.–12 p.m.) pre-school class a week each. I will teach one of these classes and the other teachers will cover the rest of the week. All candidates must have children between the ages of two and five who will be students in the at-home pre-school. All candidates must be able to offer a classroom location on the day of the week they teach. Teachers can enroll up to two children and expected class size is between five and ten. Teachers cover the cost of the supplies for the day of the week that they teach; otherwise, classes are free.

parents that get together once a month to share curriculum, ideas, and resources. If you plan to home-school your child on your own, you can still be part of a pre-school co-op. What's important to recognize is that the main benefit of creating or joining a co-op is that your child will be around other children. What all school co-ops have in common is intensive parent involvement, a group of children, and a trusted, supportive community.

How to create your pre-school co-op

✳ Choose a model that is good for you.

✳ Send out an outreach email or make a flyer that corresponds to the model you have chosen.

✳ Interview candidates and choose the most suitable. Be safe—if these people are not friends or community members whom you know well, conduct background checks.

✳ Hold several meetings to determine a schedule, director, member's responsibilities, costs, and location. Co-ops run smoothly only when everyone is equally committed and invested in the outcome.

✳ Once organized, begin classes. I recommend having a one-hour teacher meeting weekly. This can be used for planning and discussing what is and is not working.

Group teaching, two days a week

I'm looking for four parents who will meet twice a week during the normal hours of their home-school day (8 a.m.–12 p.m.) to help give a diversified and social educational experience to our home-schooled children. These group teachings will supplement and enrich your home-schooling. Meeting as a group twice a week will give your child the opportunity to meet other children and have new teachers, as well as be taught unique classes as we will all bring our special skills to the table. Parents will meet once a month for a resource and idea-sharing support group. This is free unless we decide to hire specialists or need special supplies, in which case the cost will be shared and therefore affordable for parents.

Group teaching, five days a week

I'm looking for four parents to come together five days a week, 8 a.m.–12 p.m., to create a free pre-school experience for their children. Each parent would be responsible for leading one activity or lesson a day while the others assisted. Benefits include free schooling, children socialize with other children and adults, small classroom size with more adults per child, you being with your child, and much more. There will be a half-day free play for children on Fridays and teachers will meet at this time to discuss plans for the following week.

Stay-at-Home Anniversary and Date Nights

One sacrifice that all parents make is the amount of quality time spent with their significant other. This doesn't mean that your relationship has to suffer. My husband and I are a stronger couple than we've ever been. In this section, I will give you some ideas for great stay-at-home date nights, but first I want to mention what I believe is at the heart of a successful post-children partnership.

Our success has been due to splitting everything 50/50. Gender roles go out the window; supporting each other when things get tough takes priority. We're open communicators, we respect each other, we make sure we both have some time alone each day, and if one of us is feeling taxed, the other lovingly steps in. We have a set schedule and have invented ways to split childcare, working, and house duties.

And while all of this helps, of the utmost importance is cultivating a true appreciation for the other. While some degree of traditional romance is sacrificed, we stay connected via a deeper and daily exchange of love and appreciation for the other's efforts. Believing that your partner is always looking out for you and contributing however he/she can is a powerful tool in keeping conflicts at bay, as is sharing the feeling of joy that comes from knowing that you are fantastic parents. Being an Attachment Parent is all consuming, but I believe it can help you

to bond with your partner as much as with your child.

Needless to say, there will be times when you appreciate remembering what your bond was like when it was just to the two of you; to fulfill that desire, many parents try to schedule date nights. Scheduling can be tricky. As APs, many of us get so accustomed to being with our children all day that leaving them for an evening feels unnatural. Some of us would love to get out for the night, but our little one doesn't do well with a babysitter or our babysitter cancels. If this year is going to be a stay-at-home anniversary for you, here are three ideas for how you can spend your special day, followed by fun ways to spend a date night with your significant other at any time of year.

Make a relationship collage

Compile a list of love letters, birthday cards, wedding photos, pictures that capture special events or important family accomplishments, and small trinket keepsakes that can be attached to a collage. Visit your local craft store and pick up an antique-style thick corkboard, some ribbon, and other collage-making decorations.

Once you have all of the supplies you need, create a collage together. You'll end up talking about what to put up and why, you'll go down memory lane and rediscover your appreciation and love for each other. Remember, you have to agree on everything that goes on the collage, so there is a lot of discussion involved. Not only is the result a gorgeous wall hanging for your home, but the process involves a great deal of reflection on the positive aspects of your relationship. Make sure to top this date off with your favorite take-out and chocolates.

Make life goals

Buy a beautiful journal that you can use for jotting down ideas and aspirations that you and your partner have for your future. On your anniversary, discuss your visions for the future with each other. Ask yourselves, what would we like to accomplish together? What are we doing right now that is right? What are we doing right now that doesn't feel right? What goals can we make for our future? Ask your partner if there is anything you can do better or differently in your relationship to make him or her happy. Write your list in such a way as to reflect both short- and long-term goals.

Plan your next vacation

This is only fun if you plan all of the details. It won't take much time for the two of you to agree on a vacation spot. What makes this idea fun is to choose a date, pick a hotel, print off the map, circle the attractions you plan to visit, and estimate the overall cost. Is this a mini trip to your local beach six months from now or that trip to Paris you swear you're going to take in five years? Whatever it is, commit to doing it. If you're both invested in believing that this trip is really going to happen the way it is being planned, then it will be exciting and romantic. Make hot chocolate and exchange foot massages.

Date-night ideas

* Complete an overdue house project (chalk-board cabinets.)
* Make a fancy dessert (raspberry cheese Danish, baklava, cinnamon rolls.)
* Plan a weekend vacation.
* Grab take-out sushi and rent a movie.
* Begin reading a novel together.
* Make a collage of your dream house.
* Order a pizza and watch YouTube videos.
* Make ice cream sundaes.
* Make a collage of your dream garden.
* Bake bread.
* Play board games.
* Write a book together.
* Shop for something online that you both want.
* Write a blog post on your family blog (or start a family blog.)
* Have a yoga night.
* Learn something new together (instrument, jewelry making, sprouting.)
* Make a list of things that will simplify life; practice them for that week.
* Read a relationship book; practice a few tips from it for that week.
* Paint a picture together or paint separately but at the same time.
* Create a home-schooling lesson for your little one.
* Exchange salon services at home.
* Make a clay sculpture together.

Concluding Words

Being a new parent is an incredibly trying experience. It's similar to being a new employee in a career that you're genuinely excited but anxious about. Except, imagine that you're a new employee for a company that you hope to retire with, you've had no training, and you've been put in the position of C.E.O. Suddenly, everyone you work with is looking to you for the answers and the whole operation depends on you. That's what new parenthood is like.

You have to take care of your child and you have to do it while you're learning how to take care of your child. This dilemma is true for any parent, but I'd argue that AP parents don't have the myriad of helpful resources that other parents have to guide them in their journey. The frustration I felt was due to losing countless hours searching for answers; I browsed forums, articles, and books, and often came away with less than I needed. Throughout all of this advice seeking, I learned AP mothers sometimes had to defend their parenting choices in situations where they were only asking for advice. I learned that not all of my friends would agree with my parenting style and instead of doing our best to support one another, we would end up speaking defensively on parenting matters.

One of my dear friends was quite offended when I suggested that AP might actually be the cause of some difficult behaviors in our children; when I gently reminded her that she had

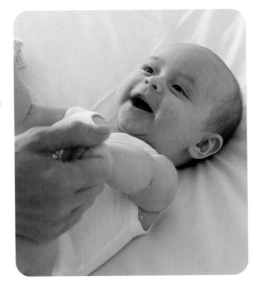

called me in complete anxiety, doubting her decision to AP because of how clingy (aka attached) her child was, she began to see the truth of my words. She then confided in me that her defensiveness was due to thinking that AP mothers should not share this kind of information for fear that it might dissuade other moms from going AP.

Someone finally said what I knew many AP mothers were saying: "We must protect AP's good image by being AP warriors." I don't buy that. The warrior image is precisely what many other types of parents dislike about AP. On good days we have a tendency to feel proud, on bad days we have a tendency to give up. There has to be something in between. That's what I hope this book is.

If I met my goals with this book, you've learned that everyday parenting challenges, such as bath time, night-weaning, and creating a sleep schedule will be unique for an AP parent. We don't practice baby training. We practice gentle, often child-led parenting methods with patience. AP parents need a book that gives them advice on how to do the basic parenting things the AP way. You've also learned that AP-specific practices, such as co-sleeping and babywearing, may be perfectly natural but not perfectly easy. I hope I've given you support and confidence via practical advice. I also hope I sent the message that, although AP is draining, a bit of creativity can go a long way in making your

child happier. Also, it is helpful to keep plans, stay organized, and try new things.

A helpful guide

When I reflect on writing this book, I remember those moments when I compiled lists that made me feel a bit hypocritical. It is impossible to practice all of these tips all of the time. If you follow one tip per list you will be a better parent. This isn't an all-or-nothing type of text; it's simply a guide. I also felt a huge sense of relief in writing this book. This was a chance for me to take hours and hours of research, organize it, and share it. Most of what I found seemed inaccessible, too long, redundant, and always missing the essence. In writing this book, I felt I was given the opportunity to share the essence of many great parenting techniques out there and this alone has been rewarding.

When I was working on the introduction to this book, I found that my breath would shallow. This may sound a bit dramatic, but it's true. I felt sadness for my family due to the pain we experienced at those times. I recall the fear and anxiety I had in those moments, the motivation I had to make things better and, as explained above, the frustration with the long hours put in. It was an overwhelming time for us. Did we really survive all of this? Did my husband and I really give up everything in the past three years in order to be successful AP parents to a high-need child? I don't always recognize the people that my husband and I are now, but Keli will forever know us as her protectors and allies.

I first started the Attached to Parenting blog for many of the same reasons I've given for writing this book. Now that the book is written, the purpose of the blog has changed a bit. I've now included an "Ask an AP Mom Forum" in case my readers come away with more questions. I'm also working on a second book that will begin to come together through the blog, specifically for supporting mothers who have children with food sensitivities, sensory integration disorders, autism, Chrone's disease, or celiac disease. You'll continue to find play ideas, craft ideas, school lessons, and toy reviews. Lastly, I will continue to use the blog as a place to compile my research in easy, accessible ways so that parents have a one-stop place to go for non-judgmental guidance.

AP success

I hope that through this book, you found help that is personable, safe, and practical, that you feel validated in your hardships, and inspired by your successes. Please befriend other AP mothers, stay in touch, visit "Ask An AP Mom" to receive and give advice. I appreciate all of my readers and know that it is parents like you, who are willing to seek support, who will ultimately contribute to more and more successful AP stories.

Resources

Chapter 1: Early Days
Books
Sears, William et al., *The Baby Book,* (Little, Brown, 2013, revised edition)

Sears, William and Martha, *The Fussy Baby Book* (Harper Thorsons, 2009)

Berenstain, Stan and Jan, *The Berenstain Bears' Moving Day* (Random House, 1988)

Vartabedian, Bryan, *Colic Solved* (Ballantine Books, 2007)

Websites
www.rookiemoms.com/how-to-make-a-moby-wrap/
Step-by-step instructions to make your own wrap.

www.babywearinginternational.org
Filled with useful information on the benefits of babywearing for both parent and child.

Chapter 2: Sleep
Books
Sears, William et al., *The Baby Sleep Book* (Little, Brown, 2005)

Websites
http://www.nct.org.uk/parenting/sleeping-safely-your-baby
Co-sleeping safety guidelines from the National Childbirth Trust.

http://www.askdrsears.com/news/latest-news/dr-sears-addresses-recent-co-sleeping-concerns
William Sears responds to co-sleeping concerns and sets out guidelines for safe co-sleeping.

Chapter 3: Breast-Feeding and Night-Weaning
Books
Evans, Kate, *The Food of Love* (Myriad Editions, 2008)

Sears, William and Elizabeth Pantley, *The No-Cry Sleep Solution* (McGraw-Hill, 2002)

Havener, Katherine, *Nursies When the Sun Shines* (Elea Press, 2013)

Websites
www.llli.org
La Leche League International helps mothers to breast-feed through mother-to-mother support, information, and education.

Chapter 4: Food and Nutrition
Websites
http://www.healthychildren.org/English/healthy-living/nutrition/Pages/Childhood-Nutrition.aspx
Advice from the American Academy of Pediatrics

Chapter 5: Toddler Tips
Books
Any titles from the 'Way I Feel' series by Cornelia Maude Spelman (Albert Whitman and Company).

Browne, Anthony, *How Do You Feel* (Walker, 2012)

Shields, Gillian *Sometimes I Feel Sunny* (Picture Corgi, 2012)

Mayer, Mercer, *I Was So Mad* (Golden Books, 1985)

Kirwan, Wednesday, *Nobody Notices Minerva* (Sterling, 2007)

Chapter 6: Entertaining and Educating Your Child
Books
Hanneman, Monika et al., *Gardening with Children*
(Brooklyn Botanic Garden, 2007)

Wattenberg, Jane, *Mrs. Mustard's Baby Faces*
(Chronicle Books, 2007)

Sirett, Dawn, *Sophie La Girafe: Colors*
(Dorling Kindersley, 2013)

Parr Todd, *Feelings Flash Cards*
(Chronicle Books, 2010)

Chapter 7: Being a Stay-at-home Parent
Websites
www.home-school.com
Advice and tips on setting up a home school, plus
links to home-school groups around the world.

Picture credits

Vanessa Davies: 27, 34, 35, 49, 51, 73, 92.
Dan Duchars: 62
Tara Fisher: 91, 93, 94 (above and left), 95.
Emma Mitchell: 6, 8, 9, 12, 13, 14, 15, 16, 18, 19, 20, 22, 23, 38, 48, 50, 53, 59 (below), 69, 70, 71, 77, 107, 121, 130, 138, 141.
Penny Wincer: 10, 11, 24, 25, 26, 32, 36, 39, 40, 42, 45, 47, 52, 54, 55, 56, 58, 59 (above), 60, 65, 66, 74, 76, 78, 79, 82, 84, 85, 87, 88, 89, 90, 94 (below), 96, 98, 99, 100, 102, 103, 104, 108, 109, 110, 111, 115, 116, 117, 118, 120, 122, 125, 127, 129, 131, 133, 134, 135, 136, 143, 144, 146, 147, 149, 154, 155, 157.

Index

Acknowledgments

I cannot express enough gratitude to my editor,
Lauren Mulholland, for her support, encouragement,
and patience throughout the editing process.

The completion of this book would not have been
possible if it weren't for my family. My husband,
Gaura Rader, spent many dedicated hours with our
daughter to give me the necessary time for writing.
Perhaps of greater importance was his constant
enthusiasm and faith in my ability to produce something
that others would find valuable. I want to give a special
thanks to my daughter Keli whom I love endlessly.
Without her, I would never have the impetus to strive for
perfection in any area of my life.

Finally, to my grandparents for being so loving and caring
since the beginning and having an almost mystical faith
in every endeavor I embark upon as an adult. My
grandfather, in one of his many attempts to support my
passions, bought me a gardening book from CICO Books
when I was still in college. This is the very book I flipped
open when I was searching for a publisher for this book.
In the truest sense, I could not have published
this book without him.

My heartfelt thanks.
Lacie Rader